CW00549299

the immaterial

THE FRENCH LIST

the immaterial
knowledge, value and capital

ANDRÉ GORZ

TRANSLATED BY CHRIS TURNER

LONDON NEW YORK CALCUTTA

Seagull Books 2010

First published in France as *L'Immateriel* by André Gorz
Copyright © Editions Galilée 2003

English language translation copyright © Chris Turner 2010
First published in English by Seagull Books 2010

ISBN-13   978 1 9064 9 761 3

British Library Cataloguing-in-Publication Data
A catalogue record for this book is available
from the British Library

Typeset by Seagull Books, Calcutta, India
Printed at Leelabati Printers, Calcutta India

I am indebted once again to Dorine,
without whom nothing would be

.

CONTENTS

1

CHAPTER ONE

Immaterial Labour

34

CHAPTER TWO

Immaterial Capital

105

CHAPTER THREE

Towards an Intelligent Society? . . .

140

CHAPTER FOUR

. . . Or Towards a Post-Human Civilization?

IMMATERIAL LABOUR

HUMAN CAPITAL

We are living through a period in which several modes of production coexist. Modern capitalism, centred on the valorization of large quantities of material fixed capital, is increasingly giving way to a postmodern capitalism centred on the valorization of so-called immaterial capital, which is also termed 'human capital', 'knowledge capital' or 'intelligence capital'. This change is accompanied by new transformations of work. The simple abstract labour which has, since Adam Smith, been regarded as the source of value, is giving way to complex labour. Material productive work, measurable in units of output per unit of time, is giving way to so-called immaterial work, to which the classical standards of measurement are no longer applicable.

In the English-speaking world, they talk of a 'knowledge economy' and a 'knowledge society'. The Germans speak of a *Wissensgesellschaft*, while French authors write of a *capitalisme cognitif* and a *société de la connaissance*. Knowledge (*Wissen*, *connaissance*) is regarded here as the 'principal productive force'. Karl Marx already argued that it was going to become *die grösste Produktivkraft* (the greatest productive force) and chief source of wealth. 'Labour in the direct form',[1] measurable and quantifiable, will have to cease, as a consequence, to be the measure of wealth created. '[T]he creation of real wealth comes to depend less and less on labour time and on the amount of labour employed' and depends increasingly 'on the general state of science and on the progress of technology'.[2] '[D]irect labour and its quantity disappear as the determinant principle of production' to become 'an, of course, indispensable but subordinate moment, compared to general scientific labour'.[3] The 'production process' can now no longer be mistaken for a 'labour process'.

It is interesting to note how the Marxian terminology wavers in this connection. Marx speaks at times of the 'general state of science' (*der allgemeine Stand der Wissenschaft*), 'general social knowledge' (*das allgemeine gesellschaftliche Wissen*),[4] the 'general intellect', the 'general powers of the human head' (*die allgemeinen Mächte des menschlichen Kopfes*)[5] and 'the artistic, scientific etc. development' that individuals can acquire thanks to 'the time set free',[6] which 'in turn reacts back upon the productive power of labour'.[7] This means that the freeing of time 'for the full development of the individual' can be regarded, 'from the standpoint of the direct production process [. . .] as the production of *fixed capital*, this fixed capital being man himself'.[8] The idea of 'human capital' is already to be found, then, in the manuscripts of 1857–58.

I remarked on the way Marxian terminology wavers here, because we find a similar wavering in current economic and managerial theory, which speaks of 'the weightless economy', 'cognitive capitalism', 'knowledge as the main productive force', 'science as the engine of the economy', etc. What is meant precisely by references to knowledge and science in this context? Let us take a look at two quotations that cast a little light on the matter:

> Value has its source today in *intelligence* and *imagination*. The individual's *knowledge* (savoir) counts more than machine time. As the bearers of their own capital, human beings bear a part of the company's capital.[9]

This remarkable text does not refer to science or formal knowledge (*connaissance*) but to intelligence, imagination and experiential knowledge,[10] which together make up 'human capital'. The terminology breaks totally with cognitivism and scientism. Formal knowledge is, in effect, fundamentally different from experiential knowledge and intelligence (I shall deal with this point at length in the last chapter). It bears on formalized objectivized contents which cannot, by definition, belong to persons. It is one thing to know grammatical rules, but knowing how to speak a language is something fundamentally different. To know how to speak, you have to break with a cognitive relation to language. Experiential knowledge of this kind is made up of experiences and practices that have become intuitive 'facts' and habits, and intelligence covers the whole range of capacities that range from judgement and discernment to openness of mind and the aptitude to assimilate new formal knowledge and to combine that formal knowledge with experiential knowledge. Thus the expression '*la société de l'intelligence*' would be the best translation into French of what the English-speaking world calls 'the knowledge society'.

Here now is a second passage for consideration.
This is an extract from an address by Norbert Bensel,
the Human Resources Director of Daimler-Chrysler:

> The employees of an entreprise are part of
> its capital [. . .] The motivation and know-
> how of the employees, their flexibility,
> capacity for innovation and concern to sat-
> isfy the clients' wishes [*Kundenorientierung*]
> constitute the raw material for innovative
> service products [. . .] Their behaviour and
> their social and emotional skills play an in-
> creasing role in the evaluation of their work
> [. . .] This will no longer be assessed by the
> number of hours they put in, but on the
> basis of objectives achieved and the quality
> of outcomes. They are entrepreneurs.[11]

What strikes us from the outset here is that Bensel
is not speaking either of formal knowledge or voca-
tional skills. Among the employees of one of the
world's largest corporations, the crucial factors are
behavioural skills, expressive and imaginative abilities

and personal involvement in the task at hand. All these qualities and skills are normally regarded as specific to the providers of *personal services*, to the suppliers of an immaterial labour that is impossible to quantify, store, certify, formalize or even objectify.

TO WORK IS TO *PRODUCE ONESELF*

This is because the digitization of industry is tending to transform work into the management of a continuous information flow. The operative must 'give himself' or 'devote himself' constantly to this management of flows; he has to *produce himself* as subject to take on this role. Communication and cooperation between operatives are an integral part of the nature of the work. 'Performance depends, first and foremost, on systemic aspects and relations between individuals,' writes Pierre Veltz. 'It isn't the sum of the work of individuals that counts but the quality and aptness of the web of communications woven around the productive system.'[12] Work is no longer measurable by pre-established norms and yardsticks. 'We can no longer define tasks objectively. Performance is no longer defined in relation to tasks, but implicates persons directly.'[13] It depends on their subjective involvement, which, in managerial jargon, is also called their 'motivation'. Since the way tasks are to be accomplished cannot be formalized, neither can it be prescribed. What is prescribed is subjectivity—in other words, precisely what the operatives can alone produce in 'giving themselves' to their tasks.[14] The qualities expected of them that cannot be provided to order are discernment, the ability to cope with the unexpected and to identify and resolve problems. 'The idea of time as the measure of value no longer applies. What counts is quality of coordination.'[15]

Because it is impossible to measure individual performance and prescribe means and procedures for arriving at a particular outcome, executives have recourse to 'management by objectives'. They 'set objectives for the employees who then have to work out how to fulfil them. This is the return of work as service provision,'[16] of the *servicium* or *obsequium* owed to the person of the overlord in traditional society.[17]

We can understand, then, why there is no reference whatsoever to material work in the address by
the Human Resources Director of Daimler-Chrysler.
The provision of services—immaterial labour—is becoming the hegemonic form of work, while material
labour is relegated to the periphery of the production
process or is quite simply outsourced. It is becoming
a 'subordinate moment' of that process, even though
it remains indispensable and even dominant from the
quantitative standpoint. The heart of value-creation
is immaterial work.

It was important to show that this immaterial
work does not depend mainly on the *formal knowledge*
of those who perform it. It depends, first and foremost, on expressive and cooperative capacities that
cannot be taught, on a vivacity in the deployment of
knowledge that is part of the culture of everyday life.
This is one of the great differences between the workers of the early manufactories or the Taylorized industries and those of post-Fordism. The former
group became operational only after they had been
deprived of the practical knowledge, skills and habits

developed by the culture of everyday life, and after they had been subjected to a thoroughgoing division of labour. There is an abundant literature on this topic, including, in particular, the writings of Adam Ferguson and Andrew Ure, on which Marx drew for Chapters 14 and 15 of *Capital, Volume 1* (1867). This destruction of the everyday forms of knowledge of a labour force that was essentially rural in origin was carried on in the period 1950–70 by almost prison-style disciplinary methods. The worker had to be induced to carry out unquestioningly and with mechanical regularity the orders the industrial machinery gave him by imposing upon him the speed and rhythm of the actions he was to perform.

By contrast, post-Fordist workers have to come into the production process with all the cultural baggage they have acquired through games, team sports, campaigns, arguments, musical and theatrical activities, etc. It is in these activities outside work that their liveliness and capacity for improvisation and cooperation have been developed. It is their vernacular knowledge that the post-Fordist enterprise sets to work and exploits. Yann Moulier-Boutang refers to this 'subsumption under capital of collective work as living labour and not as the power of science and machines' as 'second-degree exploitation':

> The worker no longer presents himself as possessor only of his hetero-produced labour-power [that is to say, of predetermined capacities inculcated by the employer], but *as having produced himself and continuing to produce himself.*[18]

Similarly, Muriel Combes and Bernard Aspe write that, 'It isn't individuals who internalize the "company culture", but rather the company that now goes "outside"—that is to say, into the realm of everyone's daily life—to seek out the skills and capacities it needs.'[19]

What companies regard as 'their' human capital is, therefore, a free resource, an 'externality' that produced itself and continues to produce itself, while companies merely tap into and channel its capacity to *produce itself.* This human capital is clearly not purely individual. The production of self does not happen out of nothing. It takes place on the basis of a shared culture transmitted by primary socialization and common forms of experiential knowledge. Parents and educators and the education and training systems play a part in the development of the 'general intellect' by making accessible knowledge of both the formal and experiential kind, together with capacities for interpretation, communication and mutual understanding that make up a shared culture. It is, however, persons who have to appropriate that shared culture by subjectivizing it. Society and its mechanisms cannot produce personal subjects. They can produce and reproduce only the framework in which subjects, in the process of socializing themselves, will produce themselves through the use they make of the language, bodily expression, interpretive schemas and behaviour specific to their society. No institution can accomplish this work of learning, appropriation and subjectivation in individuals' stead. The subject is never socially given; she is—to borrow an expression used by Maurice Merleau-Ponty with regard to consciousness—given to herself as a being that has to make herself what she is. No one can exempt the subject from this task, nor force it upon her.

In becoming the foundation of a value-production based on continual innovation, communication and improvisation, immaterial labour tends, in the end, to become indistinguishable from a labour of self-production. The operatives of the network economy are the actors in a form of organization that is ceaselessly self-organizing. Their product is not a tangible thing, but, first and foremost, the interactivity that fuels everyone's activity. Each individual has to produce herself as activity to bring into being a process that is the outcome of everyone's work and exceeds the sum of the individual activities. Pierre Lévy used the image of the 'improvised polyphonic choir',[20] by which he meant an activity that adapts to, goes beyond and fuels the activity of others as it gives rise to a shared outcome.

The paradigm of the improvised polyphonic choir applies pre-eminently to Internet-based virtual communities, but it is, at least potentially, the model underlying all networked interactive work. The division of labour into specialized hierarchical tasks is virtually abolished, as is the block on producers appropriating the means of production for themselves and self-managing them. The separation between the workers and their reified work—and between this latter and its product—is, therefore, virtually abolished, it becoming possible for the means of production to be appropriated and pooled. The computer emerges here as the universal and universally accessible tool through which all forms of knowledge and all activities can theoretically be pooled. And it is, indeed, this right to free access and to shared use that are called for by the anarcho-communist Free Software and Free Network communities. The following passage from Marx and Engels' *German Ideology* inevitably comes to mind:

All earlier revolutionary appropriations were restricted; individuals, whose self-activity was restricted by a crude instrument of production and a limited intercourse, appropriated this crude instrument of production, and hence merely achieved a new state of limitation. Their instrument of production became their property, but they themselves remained subordinate to the division of labour and their own instrument of production . . . [I]n the appropriation by the proletarians, a mass of instruments of production must be made subject to each individual, and property to all. Modern universal intercourse can be controlled by individuals, therefore, only when controlled by all.[21]

At the end of this argument, Marx defined Communism as the abolition of the work—'that has lost all semblance of self-activity' and is 'robbed [. . .] of all real life-content'—of individuals who have 'become abstract individuals'.[22]

'TOTAL MOBILIZATION'

For the moment the important matter is that the activity of self-production is a necessary dimension of all immaterial labour and that such labour tends to call on the same capacities and personal dispositions as free, non-work activities. Combes and Aspe write:

> It is in this sense that we may speak of a 'total mobilization' of capacities and dispositions, including the affective [. . .] Henceforth, it is no longer possible to know when we are 'outside' what can be asked of us in work. Ultimately, it is no longer the subject cleaving to the work but rather, the work cleaving to the subject . . .

'As poor and inept as the work may be', as 'unworthy and derisory as its goals may be', it 'requires the mental and affective powers of the individual for its accomplishment', together with the individual's 'virtuosity' and 'that which defines her value in her own eyes'. It is impossible to 'sabotage' work that mobilizes our virtuosity without 'suffering contempt from oneself and from others.' Thus 'it is not clear how a "weightless" economy could function without subjecting individuals to a new form of voluntary servitude.' The question which then arises is 'how not to invest one's own dignity in an unworthy activity.'[23]

However, all large companies know that it is impossible, *within the framework of a wage-relation*, to obtain total involvement from their employees or unconditional identification with the job. By the mere fact that it is contractual, the wage-relation recognizes the difference, if not indeed separation, between the contracting parties and their respective interests. By limiting the rights of the employers and the duties of the employees to a determinate amount of work performed, it has an emancipatory character. In so doing, it marks a boundary between the sphere of work and the sphere of individual private life.

Big companies are, consequently, trying to transform the wage-relation into an associative one by offering essential employees stock options—in other words, a share in the capital and profits of the firm.

But this solution is of only limited effectiveness. The more work calls on talent, virtuosity and the capacity for self-production that 'defines the value' of the employee 'in her own eyes', the more these capacities will tend to exceed their limited deployment in a determinate task. This can provide only a contingent illustration of her talents. She will tend to convince herself that she is worth more than what she does as a career. She will invest her dignity in the unpaid exercise of her capacities outside work, which leads to journalists writing books, graphic artists creating works of high art, computer analysts demonstrating their virtuosity as hackers or as developers of free software—all ways of retaining one's honour and 'preserving' one's 'soul'. In order to withdraw a part of their lives from this all-absorbing employment, the 'workers in the immaterial economy' accord an importance that ends up surpassing that of their work to sporting, leisure, cultural or voluntary activities, in which self-production is its own end. Alain Lebaube sums up the situation perfectly: 'However brilliant they may be, the young graduates refuse to commit themselves fully to the job. They give of themselves mechanically, but hold back their souls, with that reserve possessed by the highly gifted, who are capable of "faking it".[24]

THE COMING OF THE SELF-ENTREPRENEUR

The total subsumption of self-production by capital runs up against insuperable limits, then, for at least as long as there continues to be a heterogeneity between the individual and the company—between labour-power and capital—that allows the individual to pull back and refuse all-absorbing employment. No sooner has one stated this obstacle to total subsumption than the way of by-passing it becomes apparent: the difference between the subject and the company, between labour-power and capital, must be eliminated. *People must become enterprises for themselves*; for themselves, as labour-powers, they must become a fixed capital demanding to be continually reproduced, modernized, expanded and valorized. No constraints must be imposed on them from outside; they must be their own producers, their own employers and their own sales force, obliging themselves to impose the necessary constraints on themselves that will ensure the viability and competitiveness of *the enterprise that they are*. In short, salaried employment must be abolished.

This was what Bensel was saying in his conference paper, presenting the enterprise's 'employees' as 'entrepreneurs'. As entrepreneurs not just in 'management by objectives', but also—first and foremost—whatever their status, through the management of their labour-power, now regarded as their fixed capital. Salaried employment must be abolished, announced Charles Handy and William Bridges in the early 1990s, being among the first to do so. There must be only sole-trader enterprises providing individual services. Everyone must take responsibility for their health, mobility, ability to work variable hours and the updating of their knowledge. They must manage their human capital throughout their lives, investing in it continually in the form of training, and they must understand that the possibility of selling their labour-power depends on the unpaid, voluntary, unseen work they put in continually to reproduce it anew.

Big firms will now retain only a small core of stable full-time employees. The rest of 'their' personnel—90 per cent in the case of the hundred largest American companies—will be formed from a variable mass of external collaborators, agency and temporary workers, genuinely or falsely self-employed persons, as well as high-flying professionals. The company can dump an increasing part of the costs (of the value) of their labour on to these external workers. It externalizes, at their expense, all or part of the costs of their continuing training, health insurance and pensions. It purchases their services by negotiating their prices on a task-based or sessional basis; has them compete with one another; affords itself the possibility of varying hugely the amount of work it requires from them, without needing to concern itself about their working hours and without having to recruit them, make them redundant or pay them compensation. The future belongs to the self-entrepreneurs, whose numbers are increasing rapidly in Great Britain, Italy and Sweden. A German trade union foundation has suggested that self-entrepreneurs should be 'unionized' in organizations comparable to craft guilds or employers' organizations.[25]

LIFE IS BUSINESS

With self-entrepreneurship, whole persons and entire lives can, at last, be put to work and exploited. Life becomes 'the most precious capital'. The boundary between work and non-work fades, not because work and non-work activities mobilize the same skills, but because time for living falls, in its entirety, into the clutches of economic calculation, into the clutches of value. Every activity must be able to become a business and, as Dominique Méda writes, 'the relation to oneself and to others will be conceived exclusively in financial terms.'[26] Lévy has hailed this aberrant development more eloquently than anyone:

> From now on, everyone is in business [. . .]
> Everyone will be constantly engaged in

doing business over everything: sexuality, marriage, procreation, health, beauty, identity, knowledge, contacts, ideas [. . .] We no longer know very clearly when we're working and when we're not. We'll be constantly engaged in doing all sorts of business [. . .] Even employees will become individual entrepreneurs, managing their careers as though they were a small enterprise [. . .] quick to train themselves to cope with new developments. The person becomes an enterprise [. . .] Family and nation count for nothing any more.[27]

Everything becomes a commodity. Selling oneself extends to all aspects of life. Everything is measured in money. The logic of capital, of life turned into capital, takes over all the activities and spaces in which the production of self was originally supposed to flourish as the free expenditure of energy to no other end than to develop human capacities to their highest degree. It is Lévy who is, once again, the herald of the complete subsumption of the production of self: 'The most private "personal development" will lead to greater emotional stability, a more relaxed and open way of relating, better-directed intellectual sharpness and, hence, *better economic performance*.'[28]

Such, at least, is the neo-liberal vision of the future of work: the abolition of salaried employment, generalized self-entrepreneurship, the subsumption of the whole person and the whole of life by capital, with which everyone identifies entirely.

This vision ignores the insecurity, discontinuity and randomness that now hangs over all work—over salaried employment as much as so-called freelance work. It remains silent on the fact that, in most cases, freelance workers are actually dependent on one, or a small number of, big corporations who subject them to alternating periods of hyperactivity and unemployment; and that the individuals to whom the self-entrepreneurs sell their services are themselves in a precarious position and only in a few cases—the luxury services sector being the exception—represent a clientele with solid purchasing power.

But what matter? The basic assumption of the developing 'post-employment society' is that unemployment disappears at the same time as salaried employment. If there are still people unemployed, this will simply be the sign of their deficient 'employability' and it will be for them to restore it. It is for that restoration that gaps between work, periods of unemployment and the increase in 'free time' are to serve. 'Workfare' in its Blairist version, which has eventually spread to other countries, abolishes unemployment benefit, replacing it with a 'job-seeker's allowance' and assuming that this job-seeking is the 'work' the unemployed person must necessarily perform as assiduously as possible, including by acquiring more saleable skills than she currently possesses. The obligatory production of oneself becomes a 'job' like any other.

The total 'employment' of the person is thus taken over by the state at the point where capital can no longer effect it. The omnipresent but diffuse ideologico-political constraints it places on individuals give rise to what are dubbed 'asocial' withdrawn forms of behaviour—if not indeed resistance—on the part of the latter. It was in this context that there emerged and developed the call for an unconditional, sufficient 'basic income' that would enable everyone to cope with discontinuity, intermittent working and the precariousness of work, and would also make it possible to develop independent activities, the social and/or cultural value of which cannot be measured by—or depend upon—their profitability.

THE BASIC INCOME: TWO CONCEPTIONS

Two conceptions of the basic income are, in fact, current—sometimes in one and the same writer. There is the conception that sees it as the way of wresting life away from the commercial imaginary and the total employment model, and the conception which, by contrast, sees it as a necessary remuneration for the time outside work, which now makes a crucial contribution to the productivity of work. It must be noted that this second conception contains a very formidable trap.

Starting out from the idea that the capitalist production process derives profit from all the capacities, skills and resources that people develop in their everyday life, it takes the view that the whole of life has become productive *as the production of human fixed capital.* The entirety of the production of self is thus reduced to economic work. This latter is regarded as defining it objectively. Everyone contributes to social production by the mere fact of living in society and hence deserves the payment that is the basic income.

But this conception does not merely acknowledge the total 'employment' of the person—it legitimizes it. If the basic income 'remunerates' the unseen work that is a source of the productivity of visibile work, that remuneration legitimates the *demand* that unseen work should actually make visible work as productive as possible. In this way, we remain in the realm of labour-as-a-value and the realm of productivism. We concede to capital the right to demand that the development of human capacities be done from the outset with a view to the advantage companies can derive from it, and hence that it be done—as indeed the 'pluriactivity con-

tract' proposed in the Boissonat Report stipulates—
under the control of those companies.[29]

The basic income has the sense of an 'attack on
labour-as-a-value' (Combes and Aspe) only if it neither demands nor remunerates anything. In this conception, its function is, by contrast, to restrict the
sphere of value-creation in the economic sense by enabling the expansion of those activities which create
nothing that can be bought, sold, exchanged—and
hence nothing that has a value (in the economic
sense)—but only non-marketable wealth with an
intrinsic value of its own.

By freeing the production of self from the
constraints of economic valorization, the basic
income will necessarily facilitate the unconditional full
development of persons beyond what is functionally
useful for production. Only the capacities that exceed
any productive functionality, only *the culture that serves
no purpose* render a society capable of posing questions
about the changes going on within it and imprinting
a meaning on them.

The central conflict of the era of the immaterial economy is over 'the development of all human powers as such . . . not as measured on a pre-determined yardstick' (Marx);[30] over the right of universal unlimited access to knowledge and culture; and over the refusal to allow capital to appropriate either and use them for its own ends.

Notes

1 Karl Marx, *Grundrisse der Kritik der politischen Oekonomie* (Grundrisse. Foundations of the Critique of Political Economy; Harmondsworth: Penguin in association with New Left Review, 1973), p. 705.

2 Ibid., pp. 704–05.

3 Ibid., p. 700.

4 Ibid., p. 706.

5 Ibid., p. 705.

6 Ibid., p. 706.

7 Ibid., p. 711.

8 Ibid., pp. 711–12.

9 Centre des Jeunes Dirigeants d'Entreprise, *L'entreprise au XXIe siècle* (The Company in the Twenty-first Century; Paris: Flammarion, 1996). Emphasis mine [A.G.].

10 I have used the terms 'formal knowledge' and 'experiential knowledge' to render the distinction Gorz makes quite explicitly in the text (see below, pp. 41–56) between knowledge (*connaissance*) that is 'formalizable, codifiable' (and hence to some extent 'detachable' from the knowing subject and transmissible through educational institutions) and the less explicit knowledge (*savoir*) that is at once more general and has a greater organic unity to it (associated explicitly in the text with Ivan Illich's 'vernacular knowledge'). Obviously, these two categories are not mutually exclusive. From a purely logical standpoint, it must be the case, at least hypothetically, that the more 'formal' knowledge which prevails in the techno-scientific realm can be absorbed into the broader *savoirs* and competences of what Gorz, with Habermas, terms the lifeworld (*Lebenswelt*). [Trans.]

11 Norbert Bensel, 'Arbeitszeit, Weiterbildung, Lebenszeit. Neue Konzepte' (Working Hours, Continuing Education, Time for Living. New Concepts.), communication to the International Congress 'Gut zu Wissen.

Links zur Wissensgesellschaft' (Good to Know. Left-ward to the Knowledge Society), Berlin, 4–6 May 2001.

It should be noted that some of the passages presented here by Gorz do not appear in the German text currently to be found on the website of the Heinrich Böll Foundation, which organized the Congress. [Trans.]

12 Pierre Veltz, 'La nouvelle révolution industrielle' (The New Industrial Revolution), *Revue du MAUSS* 18 (2001).

13 Ibid.

14 See Maurizio Lazzarato, 'Le concept de travail immatériel: la grande industrie' (The Concept of Immaterial Labour: Large-scale Industry), *Futur antérieur* 10 (1992).

15 Veltz, 'La nouvelle révolution industrielle'.

16 Ibid.

17 The perfect example of management by objectives on a grand scale was provided by the management of Volkswagen. It offered not to move a new production unit employing 5,000 workers abroad if the union would agree to the company-level agreement governing the other units not being applied there. Instead of this agreement, which set weekly working hours at an

average of 28.8, the management proposed paying the workers 5,000 DM (€2,500) a month for a volume of production set in advance. If production fell below the set target, wages would be reduced. If it exceeded the target, bonuses would be paid. The working hours were clearly not set in advance. In autumn 2002, the trade union eventually accepted this formula, which ultimately sounded the death knell of collective bargaining.

18 Yann Moulier-Boutang, 'La troisième transition du capitalisme' (Capitalism's Third Transition) in Christian Azaïs, Antonella Corsani and Patrick Dieuaide (eds), *Vers un capitalisme cognitif* (Paris: L'Harmattan, 2000), pp. 133–50. Emphasis mine [A.G.].

19 Muriel Combes and Bernard Aspe, 'Revenu garanti et biopolitique' (Guaranteed Income and Biopolitics), *Alice* 1 (September 1998). [This journal published only two issues over two years.]

20 See Pierre Lévy, *L'Intelligence collective* (Collective Intelligence; Paris: La Découverte, 1997), pp. 75–6.

21 Karl Marx and Friedrich Engels, *The German Ideology* (London: Lawrence and Wishart, 1970), p. 93.

22 Ibid.

23 Combes and Aspe, 'Revenu garanti et biopolitique'.

24 Alain Lebaube, 'Premier travail' (First Work), *Le Monde/Initiatives* (22 January 1992).

25 See *Wege in eine nachhaltige Zukunft* (Paths to a Sustainable Future; Düsseldorf: Hans Böckler Stiftung, 2000).

26 Dominique Méda, *Qu'est-ce que la richesse?* (What is Wealth?; Paris: Aubier, 1999), p. 136. Pages 129–39 of Méda's work provide a very good critical résumé of the—mainly British—theories of generalized self-entrepreneurship.

27 Pierre Lévy, *World Philosophie* ('World' Philosophy; Paris: Odile Jacob, 2000), pp. 84–6.

28 Ibid., p. 83. Emphasis mine [A.G.].

29 See Commissariat général du Plan, *Le Travail dans 20 ans* (Work in 20 Years' Time; Paris: La documentation française, 1995). Denis Kessler, the vice president of the French employers' association, expressed astonishment in a televised debate, that 'the economy had to finance studies in philosophy, sociology and psychology when companies lacked immediately employable personnel.'

30 Marx, *Grundrisse*, p. 488.

CHAPTER TWO

IMMATERIAL CAPITAL

THE CRISIS OF THE CONCEPT OF VALUE

If it is to be more than merely a metaphor, the expression 'knowledge economy' implies some fundamental changes to the economic system. It indicates that knowledge has become the main productive force; that, as a consequence, the products of social activity are no longer chiefly crystallized labour but crystallized knowledge; and that the exchange-value of commodities, material or otherwise, is no longer determined in the last instance by the quantity of general social labour they contain but mainly by their content in terms of general information, knowledge and intelligence. It is now this latter, not abstract social labour, measurable by a single yardstick, that becomes the main social substance common to all commodities. It becomes the main source of value and profit and hence, in the view of many writers, the main form of labour and capital.

Unlike general social labour, knowledge is impossible to translate into—or measure in—simple abstract units. It is not reducible to a quantity of abstract labour of which it can be said to be the equivalent, the outcome or the product. It covers—and refers to—a wide diversity of *heterogeneous* capacities, including judgement, intuition, aesthetic sense, level of education and information, ability to learn and to adapt to unforeseen situations, which are capacities themselves brought into play by heterogeneous activities ranging from mathematical calculation to rhetoric and the art of persuasion, from techno-scientific research to the invention of aesthetic norms.

The heterogeneity of the work activities termed 'cognitive' and of the immaterial products they create and of the capacities and knowledge they involve, renders the value of both the labour-powers and their products non-measurable. The grids for evaluating work become a tissue of contradictions. The impossibility of calibrating and standardizing all the parameters of the required work gives rise to vain efforts to quantify its qualitative dimension and the definition of performance standards calculated to the second that take no account of the 'communicational' quality of the service—a quality that is, in fact, demanded.

The crisis of the measurement of labour leads, inevitably, to the crisis of the measurement of value. When the socially necessary labour-time required for production becomes uncertain, that uncertainty cannot but impact upon the exchange-value of what is produced. The increasingly qualitative and unmeasurable character of labour throws the pertinence of the notions of 'surplus labour' and 'surplus value' into crisis. The crisis of the measurement of value throws into crisis the definition of the essence of value and, as a consequence, the system of equivalences governing commodity exchange.

In the economic sense, 'value' always refers to the exchange-value of a commodity in relation to other commodities. It is essentially relative and it does not answer the question, '*What* is it worth?' but '*How much* is it worth?' It refers to the various quantities of diverse commodities for which a quantum of a determinate commodity is exchangeable. It refers to the *relation of equivalence* of commodities to each other. It defines each commodity as exchangeable for all others in determinate proportions through their relation of equivalence. This relation is expressed in units of a yardstick-commodity for which all commodities are exchangeable at any time, and which is exchangeable for all of them—money. Money, like other commodities, has worth by virtue of its exchange-value—its 'purchasing power'. Similarly, labour-power is a commodity whose value is that of the commodities for which it is exchanged to ensure its (re)production.

The concept of value in the economic sense of exchange-value applies then only to commodities or, in other words, to goods and services that were *produced for purposes of commodity exchange*. Things that were not produced by human labour and, to an even greater degree, that are not producible, together with those things that are not exchangeable or intended for exchange, have no 'value' in the economic sense. This applies, for example, to natural riches, like the sun or the rain that are neither producible nor appropriable; and it applies, in principle, to those goods that are common to all and cannot either be divided or exchanged for something else, such as the cultural heritage. It is true, however, that though they cannot be appropriated and 'valorized', natural riches and common goods can be confiscated through the creation of artificial barriers that reserve the enjoyment of them to those who pay for a *right of access*. It is possible, through the privatization of routes of access, to transform natural riches and common goods into quasi-commodities that will earn a rent for the sellers of the access rights. Control of access is, as we shall see, a preferential form for the conversion of immaterial wealth into capital.

The question of the 'value' of experiential and formal knowledge must be considered in the light of the foregoing remarks. Experiential knowledge is an integral part of the cultural heritage; it consists of shared skills that are part of everyday life. It is on the basis of these shared skills that attested professional skills are built which, for their part, are produced for the purpose of trade in services as commodities. As for formal knowledge, it is the product of the 'universal intercourse between human beings' or, in other words, of non-commodity interaction and communication. Thomas Jefferson, in his day, said that such knowledge 'did not lend itself to private appropriation' or to commercial exchange, since it is impossible to reduce it to a measurable, shared social substance, such that one could determine relations of equivalence between its different manifestations. A market in (formal) knowledge in which items of knowledge would be traded at their 'value' is unthinkable. Since it cannot be expressed in units of value, its evaluation as capital remains problematical.

This irreducibility of formal knowledge is going to be a source of economic difficulties, incoherence, sleight of hand and misrepresentation, since there can be no question for capital of not treating (formal) knowledge—and not making it function—*as though* it were capital. There can be no question for capital of not attempting to appropriate, valorize and subsume a productive force which, in itself, cannot be reduced to the categories of political economy. It will therefore do everything within its power to 'capitalize' it, to make it correspond to the essential conditions by which capital functions and exists as capital. To be specific, knowledge must save more work than it cost to produce and must subject the work by which it is implemented to its control; it must become the exclusive property of the firm that valorizes it by incorporating it into the commodities that firm produces.

But before we examine how knowledge, formal and experiential, can function as immaterial capital, we have to define more precisely what distinguishes the two.

EXPERIENTIAL KNOWLEDGE, VALUE AND CAPITAL

Knowledge of the experiential kind is, first and foremost, a practical ability, an expertise that does not necessarily involve formalizable, codifiable knowledge. Most bodily skills lie beyond the possibility of formalization. They are not taught but are learned through practice and experience—that is to say, by practising doing what one is trying to learn to do. The transmission of such knowledge consists in appealing to the subject's ability to produce herself. This applies to both sports and to manual skills and the arts. Such practical knowledge is learned when the person has incorporated it into herself to the point of forgetting that she once had to learn it.

It is the same with the unwritten rules that govern social interactions and interpersonal relations. Like the grammatical rules that govern the workings of language, they are put into practice without being known in propositional terms and before being actually formalized. The important point here is that the *path from experiential knowledge*—expertise, know-how— *to the formal knowledge* of the laws, rules and procedures involved in it *is much shorter than the opposite pathway*. Someone who tries to learn a language, for example, by learning its grammatical rules will not be able to speak that language, whereas the person who first trains herself to speak the language will have no difficulty learning its grammatical rules by delving into the operation of that language which she *knows experientially without knowing it formally*.

A culture is the richer when the common forms of experiential knowledge out of which it is woven enable it to incorporate new formal knowledge and transform it into experiential knowledge. (I shall come back to this in the last part of this work.) Conversely, the more a society codifies its shared experiential knowledge and transforms it into formalized knowledge, the poorer its culture becomes. During the second half of the twentieth century, an endlessly expanding range of shared forms of experiential knowledge—Ivan Illich termed this 'vernacular' knowledge—was transformed into officially sanctioned professionalized knowledge and turned into services with a price on them. The rise of such professionalization disqualified those practices and relationships based in shared forms of experiential knowledge, substituting for them the paid performance of work and commercial relations.

However, professionalization is not able to translate into formal knowledge and officially sanctioned procedures—or even into science—the totality of forms of practical knowledge drawn on by professionals. A significant *remainder* of such skills escapes formalization to a greater or lesser degree. It is to the extent that it cannot be entirely taught or reduced to formalizable knowledge that professional service retains the stamp of the person providing it. Professional service is, in fact, the exploitation of a skill in the only form that can objectivize it: the form of the acts that demonstrate it. The production of these acts necessarily involves an element of self-production and of the giving of oneself. This is entirely obvious in relational services (education, care or assistance), but it is also manifest in arts and crafts, in fashion, design or advertising.

The value of a service is, therefore, the less measurable for the fact that it involves a greater element of giving of—or producing—oneself; for the fact that its incomparably personal character confers an intrinsic value on it that overrides its normal exchange-value. At the extremes, personal expertise transcends the norm of professional skills and appears as an *art* performed by a virtuoso, the person's name then equating with a brand name or company name. The services performed, being neither measurable nor comparable, become the source of a monopoly rent.

The shared experiential knowledge and skills drawn on in immaterial labour exist only in and through the living practice of them. They were not acquired or produced for the purpose of using them in work or producing value with them. They cannot be detached from the social individuals who practice them, evaluated in terms of any monetary equivalent or bought and sold. They are the product of the shared experience of life in society and cannot be legitimately equated with fixed capital. In a pioneering work, Christian Marazzi speaks in this connection of a 'new fixed capital' that has none of the traditional characteristics of fixed capital; it cannot be appropriated, divided up or quantified and remains diffuse: 'The new fixed capital is made up from the whole set of social and lived relations, from the modalities of the production and acquisition of information which, sedimenting down into the labour force, are then activated throughout the production process.'[1] And outside the production process too, it must be added. This 'new fixed capital' is not accumulated labour and cannot assume the 'value' form. It is, in its essence, social and common to all.

FORMAL KNOWLEDGE, VALUE AND CAPITAL

The question of the relationship between formal and experiential knowledge is decisive from the societal and cultural standpoint. Can formal knowledge be assimilated into experiential knowledge and incorporated into the common culture? Or, instead of expanding and fuelling that culture, does it cause it to wither away? The answer depends on both the orientation and the contents of (propositional) knowledge-production and the capacity of the common culture to give it meaning.

The history of industrialization can be read as the history of the growing divorce between the development of scientific and technical knowledge and the common culture. The systematic character of this divorce emerges clearly from the history of manufacture and of the 'automatic factory' which Marx sketches, borrowing copiously from Ferguson, Ure and William Thompson, in Chapters 14 and 15 of *Capital, Volume* 1. We find there the following quotation from Thompson:

> The man of knowledge and the productive labourer come to be widely divided from each other, and knowledge, instead of remaining the handmaid of labour in the hand of the labourer to increase his productive powers [. . .] has almost everywhere arrayed itself against labour. Knowledge [becomes] an instrument capable of being detached from labour and opposed to it.[2]

And we may take the following formula from Ferguson: 'And thinking itself, in this age of separations, may become a peculiar craft.'[3] Marx himself wrote in *Grundrisse*:

> As a productive force independent of labour, assigned to the service of capital, science [. . .] acts upon [the worker] through the machine as an alien power, as the power of the

machine itself. The appropriation of living labour by objectified labour [. . .] which lies in the concept of capital, is posited, in production resting on machinery, as the character of the production process itself [. . .] The worker appears as superfluous to the extent that his action is not determined by [capital's] requirements [. . . He is] a mere living accessory of this machinery.[4]

Techno-scientific knowledge is therefore, from the outset, not only *on the side of* capital as domination and subsumption of living labour by machinery but it even forms part of fixed capital as a means of extorting surplus labour. The bearers of such knowledge, the engineers, are expressly and ideologically in the camp of the owners of capital. They are 'executives' with power to command; they represent the owners and are responsible for the management and valorization of the fixed capital. Knowledge, at this stage, exists 'in the heads' of the 'officers of production' and in the tangible means of production as a constraining power on labour.[5] It does not yet exist as an 'immaterial' capital separated—and separable—from its material base and producible separately.

A first decisive step towards autonomizing the production of knowledge and 'capitalizing' it was to take place around 1880 when Carl Duisburg at Far-benfabriken Bayer industrialized research work in the chemical industry. The production of knowledge within that firm was subjected to the same hierarchi-cal division of labour, the same fragmentation of jobs, the same separation of intellectual from manual work as in manufacturing industries. The goal was the same—to reproduce in the field of knowledge-pro-duction the same triple dispossession that had enabled capital, by means of its 'manufactories', to ruin the independent craftworkers and make wage-labour the norm. The workers were dispossessed of their means of labour, of power over the nature of their work and their working conditions, and of power over their products. The means of labour became the exclusive property of capital which also determined the nature of work—and working conditions—and appropriated its products.

But in the knowledge industry, the products were not themselves commodities. The knowledge was not produced for its exchange-value but as a source of value of the commodities—the medicines—into which it was to be incorporated. Its use-value was certain; its cost-value, on the other hand, was unpredictable on account of the uncertainties of research and development and the impossibility of measuring knowledge-products in product units. As Enzo Rullani writes:

> Neither the theory of value of the Marxist tradition, nor the currently dominant liberal value-theory can deal with the process of transforming knowledge into value [. . .] The cost of production of knowledge is, in fact, highly uncertain and, most importantly, it is radically different from the cost of its reproduction. Once a first unit has been produced, the outlay required to reproduce other units tends towards zero. In no case does this cost bear any relation to the initial production cost.[6]

Clearly, these remarks apply very particularly to knowledge stored in software. It is often very expensive to develop such knowledge and transcribe it into digital form, but the software can then be reproduced in practically unlimited quantities at negligible cost. The same applied in Duisberg's day where the pharmaceutical industry was concerned—pills could be manufactured in unlimited quantities and their marginal unit cost tended towards the minimal, whatever the costs incurred in developing their active ingredient. Hence the following remark by Rullani applies to any commodity whose tangible form, produced at very low unit cost, is merely the vehicle for, or packaging of, its immaterial cognitive, artistic or symbolic content, such as genetically modified seeds:

> The exchange-value of knowledge is linked entirely to the practical ability to limit its free dissemination or, in other words, to limit by monopolistic or judicial means (patents, copyright, licences or contracts) the possibility of copying, imitating, 'reinventing' or learning the knowledge of others.

In other words, the value of knowledge does not derive from its natural scarcity, but solely from the limitations established, institutionally or *de facto*, on access to knowledge. However, these limitations only succeed in putting a temporary brake on imitation, 'reinvention' or substitutive learning on the part of other potential producers. The scarcity of knowledge, which gives it its value, is therefore artificial in nature. It derives from the capacity of a 'power' of whatever kind temporarily to limit its spread and regulate access to it.[7]

This allows us in part to make clear why and how 'cognitive capitalism functions differently from capitalism *tout court*.' It has, first, to deal with an unprecedented situation. Its main productive force, knowledge, is a product that is, in large part, the outcome of an unpaid collective activity, of a 'self-production' or 'production of subjectivity'. It is, to a large extent, 'general intelligence', shared culture, living and lived practical knowledge. It has no exchange-value, which means that it can, in theory, be shared at will, as anyone and everyone sees fit, at no charge, particularly on the Internet. But the fact is that the portion of knowledge that is not originally shared and common, namely formalized propositional knowledge—detachable from its producers and existent only because it has been formally produced—is also potentially free, since it can be reproduced in unlimited quantities and shared without having to pass through the value-form (money). It is, moreover, generally accessible, at least in theory, thanks to the Internet, which means that the main productive force and the main source of value can for the first time be put potentially beyond private appropriation.

But the real 'revolutionary' innovation lies elsewhere—formalized knowledge, separated from any product in which it has been, is or will be incorporated, can carry out a productive action, in and of itself, as software. It can *organize and manage* complex interactions between a large number of actors and variables, *design and run* machines, installations and flexible production systems—in short, play the role of fixed capital by substituting stored labour for living labour, material or immaterial. Since the marginal cost of software is either very small or even negligible, knowledge can save much more work than it cost and can do so on a massive scale that was unimaginable just a short time ago. And this means that, though it is a source of value, *it destroys vastly more 'value' than it serves to create*. In other words, it saves immense quantities of paid social labour and, as a consequence, diminishes—or even reduces to zero—the monetary exchange-value of an increasing number of products and services.

(Formalized) knowledge opens up the prospect, then, of the economy evolving towards affluence, which means also an economy in which production, requiring less and less immediate labour, distributes fewer and fewer means of payment. The (exchange-)value of products tends to diminish and to lead, sooner or later, to a decrease in the monetary value of total wealth produced, alongside a decrease in the volume of profits.

The affluent economy tends, of itself, towards a no-cost economy and towards forms of production, cooperation, exchange and consumption based on reciprocity and pooled resources as well as on new forms of currency. So-called cognitive capitalism *is* itself the crisis of capitalism.

In this situation, a twofold problem arises for the capitalist economy: the creation of an effective demand for what is produced with decreasing quantities of labour; the 'capitalization' and valorization of a product—knowledge—which capital has to appropriate, in order to prevent it from becoming a collective good, and make function as 'immaterial capital'.

That appropriation does not always need to be direct. It is enough for capital to appropriate the means of access to knowledge—particularly the means of access to the Internet—to retain control of knowledge and prevent it from becoming a plentiful collective good. Access—and the means of access—to knowledge thus become the major stakes in a central conflict. (I shall come back to this.) For the moment, it is worth our examining more closely how knowledge is transformed into immaterial capital and how the valorization of that largely fictitious capital is effected by the creation of monopoly positions. The trends pointed out by Jeremy Rifkin in *The Age of Access* (2000) are instructive in this regard.[8]

TRANSFORMATIONS OF KNOWLEDGE INTO IMMATERIAL CAPITAL
From Miracle to Mirage

Drawing on an abundant range of sources, Rifkin demonstrates the rise of a 'new economy'. He does not mean by this the 'new economy' driven by the start-up companies developing and marketing software for direct selling on the Internet but, rather, the new conception of what gives 'value' to products—that is to say, what makes them saleable at maximum profit. This maximum now depends more than ever on a firm's capacity to gain the allegiance of a client base, to have those clients buy the latest novelties without delay or great expense, and to persuade them of the incomparable 'value' of what it is offering.

The new element, as Rifkin sees it, can be
summed up as follows: the intangible dimension of
products now takes precedence over their material
reality; their symbolic, aesthetic or social value over
their practical use-value and, of course, over their
exchange-value, which it overrides. The major part of
profits is achieved on the basis of the intangible
dimension of commodities. Their 'materialization
becomes secondary from the economic point of view.'
Companies engaged in material production are relegated to the status of vassals of those firms whose
production and capital are essentially immaterial.

Thus a rapidly increasing proportion of firms
would rather hire their material fixed capital (build-
ings, plant, machines, transport equipment) than own
it. 'Use it, don't own it' is the watchword. In the USA,
one-third of machines, plant and vehicles is hired.
Eighty per cent of companies hire their infrastructure
from 2,000 specialized agencies. One-third of industries now outsource more than half of their production activities. IBM and Compaq, the two leaders in

their field, outsource the building, delivery and billing of their computers to the same firm, Ingram. Nike owns neither plant nor machinery—its activity is confined to design functions; manufacture, distribution, marketing and advertising are subcontracted out.

This externalization of production and material fixed capital isn't a mere extension of the 'lean production' and 're-engineering' of the 1990s. It is no longer merely a question of reducing the circulation time of capital as radically as possible by eliminating stock and all permanent staff except for a small core. The aim now is to impose a new division of labour—not just between the providers of labour but between companies and capitals. Material capital is abandoned to the subcontracting 'partners' of the mother firm, which assumes suzerainty over them, forcing them, through the constant revision of the terms of their contracts, to continually intensify the exploitation of their labour force. It buys the products provided by the subcontractors at very low prices and banks very high profits (in Nike's case, for example, 4 billion

USD a year on American sales alone) by selling them under its brand name. Labour and material fixed capital are downplayed and often ignored by the stock exchange, whereas the immaterial capital is valued at prices that have no measurable basis. Back in 1994, Marazzi wrote:

> No one buys a share in Apple Computers, IBM or any other company on the basis of the material goods possessed by the company. It is not the company's buildings or machinery that count, but the contacts and potential of the marketing structure and salesforce, the organizational capacity of the management and the inventiveness of its personnel.[9]

Hence, by 1999, the material capital of American industry represented only one-third of stock-market capitalization. According to a Swedish study quoted by Rifkin, in the same year the immaterial capital or 'intellectual capital' of most companies reached levels between five and sixteen times higher than their material and financial capital. Firms are generally tending to de-couple immaterial capital from the traditional forms of capital.

However, Rifkin omitted to situate these trends within the framework of the new economy that captivated the attention of the pundits until the downturn that began in 2000. The stock exchange's infatuation with 'immaterial assets', also known as 'intangibles', was, in the second half of the 1990s, the most spectacular outgrowth of an unprecedented stock-market boom. That boom was fuelled by the quantities of unemployed financial capital that re-engineering had first created, then augmented at an ever-increasing rate. That re-engineering, in which the 'IT revolution' played a crucial role, had consisted mainly in creating leaner productive structures and factors of production, covering such aspects as organization, the managerial and administrative apparatus, fixed capital, staff, direct and indirect wages costs and marketing costs. 'Leaner' costs had led to a rapid decrease in wages as a proportion of GDP and a rapid rise in profits and dividends, but not in investments.

Household purchasing power did not, in fact, increase across the board and there were fewer opportunities for profitable investment in the real economy. Growing quantities of financial capital in search of profitable employment found it, for want of anything better, in the development of credit. Banks vied with each other to lend to the so-called emerging countries, drew the Latin American countries into debt and encouraged households to buy on credit, to the point where, by the end of the 1990s, their indebtedness was growing at 4 per cent per annum and represented nearly 15 months' worth of the total disposable income of American households. Debts contracted in this way show up in the positive column of the banks' balance sheets. But everyone knows they have little chance of ever being paid off. To keep themselves from bankruptcy, the banks lend their debtors the money to pay the interest on their debts; the debts are, so to speak, recycled. But no matter, the development of consumer credit makes it possible, at least for a time, to prevent the contraction of the total payroll producing a contraction in the effective demand of households.[10]

It was in this context that the stock-market boom began in 1995. It took the Dow Jones index 30 years to rise from the 1,000 level to 4,000. It reached the 8,000 mark in July 1997 and 11,000 in July 1999. After encouraging households to consume the future income from their future work, capitalism quotes the future profits of future growth on the stock exchange and thereby creates an illusion of enrichment and 'value-creation' at an unprecedented pace. The increase in the fictive value of shares shows up in the balance sheets of banks and individuals, enabling the latter to borrow and the former to lend more, all of it underpinned by nothing. One-third of households borrow from their banks to buy more shares which they will pay for with part of their stock-market gains.

Media-savvy economists believe they have discovered the goose that lays the golden egg. An American investment fund manager announces that, in 2079, the Dow Jones will reach 750,000. Official experts, ministers and the leaders of big corporations assert that the continually rising stock market will make it possible to fund future pensions, so long as employees invest in shares. No one envisages that the stock market could turn, nor that it will necessarily fall when the number of retirees, as sellers of shares, exceeds the number of buyers.

When the stock-market valuation of companies comes to exceed their tangible assets by a factor of 100, things begin to seem astonishing. But no matter, material fixed capital isn't everything. There is also immaterial, intangible capital which is impossible to evaluate and is, moreover, the key to growth and future profits. So let us de-couple the intangible from the tangible and quote them separately on the stock exchange. The boom in intangibles can go on accelerating. And their valuations can never seem too high because intangibles have no assessable value.

The Nasdaq led the way here. Everyone got in on the act. What is a start-up worth? What is Microsoft worth? Any price you like. The initial investment is of little consequence—it may be as little as one or two PCs, the renting of a room where two friends have spent a couple of weeks or six months writing software that will save its users time and money. What counts is originality, efficiency and reliability. And the costs are not necessarily in the labour of invention, but in what it takes to sell the invention before others have discovered—or managed to copy—what you have done. All in all, the costs lie mainly in *transforming the invention into a commodity and bringing it to market as a patented branded product.*

The stock-market value of the invention will essentially reflect supposed future profits. The immateriality of intellectual capital makes it best suited to function as a promise of unlimited future markets for commodities of a non-measurable value and, hence, as a promise of unlimited stock-market gains. Provided, of course, that this capital is protected property and occupies a monopoly position.

The de-coupling of immaterial from material capital takes place, then, in a context in which the mass of fictive capital has already flown free of the real economy and has begun, on the derivatives market, to make money by buying and selling nothing but fictive money hundreds of times a day. The fiction outstrips reality and is seen as more real than real until the—unpredictable, but inevitable—day the bubble bursts.

The implosion began in 2000 and, in less than two years, produced the biggest crash since 1929. The collapse of the intangibles market reflects the intrinsic difficulty of assigning a monetary equivalent—a 'value'—to assets that are not exchangeable on the market, assets that are not divisible or measurable and hence of no convertible exchange-value. This difficulty is quite simply the intrinsic difficulty of making intangible capital function as capital, of making so-called cognitive capitalism function as capitalism.

I don't mean to imply by this that, at bottom, nothing has changed. On the contrary, so-called cognitive capitalism *is* the crisis of capitalism. It seeks to find a way out of that crisis by clever devices. We must recall, first, that the stock-market boom of the latter half of the 1990s was already a crisis symptom. A growing quantity of unemployed financial capital sought refuge on Wall Street, rocketing up share prices, demanding unprecedented yields and hastening the reduction of wage costs in the name of 'shareholder value'. The rising stock exchange became a money-making machine: while 80 per cent of wage-earners were growing poorer, a good third of households were gripped by a consumer-credit frenzy—their increasing share capital enabled them to borrow uninterruptedly from their banks, to transform their fictive capital into a real income, entirely disconnected from work of any kind. It was as though the Central Bank were putting into circulation a consumption money reserved for the better-off third of the population, a money intended to preserve the system from a crisis of under-consumption.

Inevitably, then, a downturn on the stock exchange will produce a very appreciable contraction of effective demand and a long deep recession or depression, unless the lesson has been learned—only a specific consumption money (different from the money that currently fulfils four very different functions), a money created and distributed according to political criteria and one that is by nature non-inflationary (of limited duration and circulation), can avert the implosion of a system that produces more and more commodities while distributing fewer and fewer means of payment. It is very probable that such a money will be introduced in the next 20 years, in various disguises to begin with, before it will dare call itself by its name.[11] *Depending on the modalities and political context of its introduction, consumption money either will or will not be the means by which capitalism survives its own death* by rescuing the reign of the commodity and the symbolic power of money.[12]

Meanwhile, the problem of effective demand will tend to be aggravated on account of the practices whereby companies prevent the diminution of the overall volume of paid work leading to a diminution in the overall value of production and the volume of profits. How, in effect, can the immaterial, the 'cognitive', which is non-measurable and the value of which it is impossible to determine, function as capital and become the main source of value? This is a question worthy of closer examination.

Symbolic Monopolies and Monopoly Rents

We can find the beginnings of an answer in Rifkin's *The Age of Access*. Rifkin shows that material products and a growing proportion of services are dressed up as vehicles for patented 'knowledge'. That knowledge confers on the commodity a value that bears no relation to what was previously understood as 'economic (exchange-)value'—namely, a quasi-artistic value, symbolic of that which is inimitable and has no equivalent.

The production, sale and leasing of licensed commercial images and trading names is becoming a powerful thriving industry. The production and leasing of know-how, to which a specific brand label can attach itself, are breaking free of the implementation of that know-how. This is now leased for its exclusive image in the operation known as franchising.

Franchising is current both in services (among other sectors, fast food) and in the textile, pharmaceutical and mechanical industries, etc. Franchising is simply the privatization of forms of knowledge or know-how patented under a brand name, the *use* of which is leased out to the companies that implement it. The mother firm remains the sole proprietor of that knowledge and know-how. It sets its knowledge to work as (immaterial) capital through the intermediary of the franchisees. That capital functions as fixed capital insofar as it contributes to the productivity of the licensed companies, organizes their work and controls them remotely. The whole of the mother company's profits will come from the rental charges it collects from the franchisees. These charges are, in fact, monopoly rents and may represent a multiple of the cost of the 'cognitive capital' held by the mother firm.

We may say, paraphrasing Rullani, that the value of an item of knowledge 'is entirely linked to the capacity to monopolize the right to use it'. Similarly, when it comes to commodities with a high immaterial content, instead of saying that 'their value has its source in knowledge' it would be truer to say it has its source in the monopoly of knowledge, in the exclusiveness of the qualities which that knowledge confers on the commodities that embody it, and in the firm's capacity to preserve that monopoly. This capacity will depend on how quickly the firm manages to innovate, bring its innovations to market and outpace and overtake its competitors. 'Intellectual property' as well as 'company secrecy' become imperative. Without them there is no 'knowledge capital'.

Monopolizing knowledge, know-how and concepts remains, however, a difficult task—it requires financial investment that is often much higher than that required to produce the underlying knowledge. This is true even in the pharmaceutical and software industries. Microsoft, for example, devotes around one-third of its turnover to advertising and marketing; the design, development and production of new products absorb another third and profits represent a more or less equivalent figure. The immaterial capital of companies like Nike, Coca-Cola or McDonald's consists mainly in the monopoly power they exert over the market—a power symbolized by their brand names—and the magnitude of the rents this power provides. The brand is already a capital in itself, insofar as its prestige and celebrity confer a *convertible symbolic value* on the products that bear its name. Its fame is not in fact due to the intrinsic qualities of its products alone—it has had to be built up through significant investment in marketing and recurrent advertising campaigns. It is these that have constructed a brand *image* endowing the products with a *distinctive identity* and alleged qualities on which the firm claims a monopoly.

The pursuit of monopoly rents becomes all the more obsessive as the increased productivity of labour reduces the volume of profits companies can derive from exploiting a constantly decreasing workforce. The fall in the volume of profits to be made on material commodities probably explains the other trend highlighted by Rifkin—industry's tendency no longer to *sell* its products but to *lease* them to its clients, and hence transform *buyers* into *users*. This way, firms cease to be mainly manufacturers and become mainly *service providers*, guaranteeing the use-value and maintenance of the products leased. The firm thus remains in permanent relations with its customers. It can encourage them to replace the equipment they hire with new models and to combine leasing with the purchase of additional services. Direct permanent access to users reduces the time taken bringing products to market and saves a significant proportion of advertising costs.

But the development of leasing does not simply speed up the circulation of capital. It does not tend merely to make clients captives of the firm. It also tends to make up for the rapid decline in personnel employed in production, and hence the decline in its value and profitability. The largest part of surplus-value must increasingly be produced by a large service personnel. The outsourcing or 'externalization' of material production is accompanied by an *internalization* of the service provision that companies had previously abandoned to independent firms. With this internalization, they kill two birds with one stone—increasing the number of staff capable of producing surplus-value and rationalizing the services provided, to the point where the rate of surplus-value produced is far higher than that achieved in material production. Material products finally become 'vehicles' for the services sold.

These services bring the firm profits that are all the higher for the fact that their apparent personalization succeeds in masking the reality of their standardization. We should remember here the words of the Human Resources Director at Daimler-Chrysler—the work of the staff will be assessed not by the number of hours, but by the 'behaviour and social and emotional skills' and 'concern to satisfy the clients' wishes [*Kundenorientierung*]' that 'employees' show.[13] For the buyer, the quality of the service counts more than its price as long as that quality is 'incomparable'. The purchasers of services with a high relational component acquire them for their use-value, not as a function of their exchange-value (their price).

The notion of socially necessary labour time ceases
to be relevant for services that are personal in appearance. The seller must make the client forget that
selling is his aim and must, by treating the client as an
individual, disguise the commercial relationship as a
private one to which economic logic does not apply. The
value of personal services ceases to be measurable as
these services lose their character of social labour.

This apparent personalization of the relationship
between service providers and clients is, in reality,
merely the concrete illustration of the personalization
of the relationship that the firm itself seeks to establish with its clientele. In that relationship, the service
providers act, in effect, as personal representatives of
the firm. It is not they who lend the firm their per-
sonalities but the very opposite—the personality of
the firm expresses itself through them. They have the
style, behaviour and language of the 'company'. The
company confers their identity on them in the same
way that it aims to confer an inimitable identity on the
clients of its brand. The production of brand-images

is the most flourishing and profitable sector of the immaterial industry and the source of the largest monopoly rents.

The production of brand-images and the marketing, advertising, styling and design industry that underpins it do, however, fulfil a dual function: they have a properly economic and commercial function on the one hand; and a political, cultural function on the other. From the economic point of view, the brand must endow the product with a non-measurable symbolic value that takes precedence over its utilitarian value and exchange-value. It must render the branded article non-interchangeable with articles intended for the same use and endow it with a social and expressive artistic or aesthetic value. The brand must function like the signature of a famous artist, attesting that the object is not a common-or-garden commodity but a rare incomparable product. It bestows upon the product a symbolic value that is the firm's monopoly and that withdraws it, at least temporarily, from competition.

This symbolic monopoly can persist only if the firm reproduces it continually through advertising campaigns and innovations that regenerate the exclusivity and scarcity of what it offers. The symbolic qualities have continually to be adjusted to changes in taste and fashion, and those changes have to be maintained in such a way as to renew, extend and increase the value of the product, consumer motivation and available outlets. And this goes for yoghurts, washing powder and frozen ready-meals as much as it does for so-called consumer durables and genuine fashion articles, on which advertising and marketing expenditure can reach more than 40 per cent of company turnover.

Insofar as the symbolic value of the product becomes the main source of profit, value-creation shifts to a terrain where productivity gains can continue to have little impact on price levels. The immaterial fixed capital of the company now includes its fame and prestige, constitutive of a symbolic capital, and the talent, know-how and creativity of the staff who produce the quasi-artistic dimension of the goods.

The Production of the Consumer

However, viewing matters more closely, immaterial fixed capital is put to work on a quite other level—it functions as a means of producing consumers. It functions, in other words, to produce wishes, desires, self-images and lifestyles which, once adopted and internalized by individuals, transform them into that new species of buyers 'who have no need of what they desire and no desire for what they need'. This is the definition of the *consumer* as conceived or, more properly, invented by Edward Bernays, a nephew of Sigmund Freud, in the early 1920s.

Bernays had settled in the USA at a point when industrialists were wondering how they could find civilian outlets for the enormous production capacities that industry had developed during the First World War. How were buyers to be found for all that industry could produce? Bernays had the answer. He had developed a new discipline—'public relations'. First in articles, then in books, he set about explaining that although people's *needs* were limited by nature, their *desires* were in essence unlimited. To expand those desires, all that was needed was to get rid of the false idea that individuals' purchases corresponded to practical needs and rational considerations. It was unconscious and irrational motivations that had to be appealed to—fantasies and unavowed desires. Instead of addressing itself to the buyers' practical good sense, as it had in the past, advertising should contain a *message* that transformed even the most mundane products into vehicles of symbolic meaning. The aim had to be to appeal to 'irrational emotions', to create a consumer culture and produce the archetypal consumer who would seek and find in consumption a means of expressing her or his innermost self or, as a 1920s' advert had it, 'what is most precious and unique about you, but remains hidden'.

When the tobacco industry approached Bernays and asked him whether he could see a way to get women to smoke, he took up the challenge without hesitation. The cigarette, he explained, was a phallic symbol, and women would begin to smoke if they came to see cigarettes as a way of emancipating themselves symbolically from male domination. The press was alerted that, on the occasion of the great Fourth of July Parade in New York, a sensational event would take place. And in fact, when the signal was given, some 20 young debutantes pulled cigarettes and lighters out of their handbags and lit their symbolic 'torches of freedom'. The cigarette had become the symbol of women's emancipation. Bernays—and the tobacco industry—had won.

'You have [. . .] transformed people into self-perpetual happiness machines,' President Herbert Hoover told Bernays in 1928. For his part, Bernays was entirely aware of having transformed citizens who represented a potential threat to the established order into docile consumers: the governing classes, he believed, would be able to do as they wished so long as they were able to channel the interests of the population towards—and through—the individual desire to consume.[14]

The consumer, who is individual by definition, was thus conceived from the outset as the opposite of the citizen, as the antidote, so to speak, to the collective expression of collective needs, the desire for social change and the concern for the common good. The advertising industry constantly fulfilled a dual—economic and political—function by appealing not to the imagination and desires of *all* but to the imagination and desire of *each* as a private person. It does not promise potential buyers an improvement in their shared condition. It promises, rather, that each person can escape the common condition by becoming the 'happy privileged individual' who is able to buy herself some new, scarce, improved, distinctive item. It promotes the pursuit of individual solutions to collective problems. The market is supposed to be able to solve these, without encroaching upon the sovereignty and self-interest of each individual. Advertising calls on all individuals, insofar as they *are* social individuals, to reject their social existence. It is an *antisocial socialization*.[15]

As a production of imagination, desires and sensibility—in short, of subjectivity—advertising is ostensibly of the order of artistic creation. But it is creation in a state of serfdom, in the service of the commodity. The aim of the advertiser's art, like the aim of the propaganda of totalitarian regimes, isn't to banish the clichés, stereotypes and commonplaces in which our sensibilities tend to become mired. Its object is primarily to sell commodities transfigured into works of art by the propagation of aesthetic, symbolic and social norms that must be fleeting and ephemeral, the intention being that they should give way, before very long, to new norms.

Artistic creation must *be disturbing*, in order to refresh our ways of seeing and our imaginative capacities. Advertising and fashion have to *please the eye* and impose their norms. As a privileged vehicle of those norms, the brand image effects *a seizure of power* by immaterial fixed capital over public space, the culture of everyday life and the social imaginary. As the instrument by which the commodity is to be able to produce its consumers, the firm's symbolic capital gets itself developed and enhanced by those consumers themselves. It is they who will carry out the *invisible labour* of self-production that 'provides the object with a subject' or, in other words, produces within each of them the wishes, desires and self-images that the commodity is supposed adequately to express. In short, brand advertising induces in the consumer a self-production that valorizes branded products as emblems of her own valorization. It is through the power it assumes over this invisible work of self-production, through the veiled violence that the invasion of all the spaces and moments of daily life by advertising exerts on the individual, that symbolic capital really functions as a fixed capital.

In the end, we find the same self-subjugation in the field of consumption as we saw in the field of work. The inducement consumers receive to produce themselves in a form commensurate with the self-image held out by advertising and to change their borrowed identity as tastes and fashions change, prepares them to produce themselves in their work in conformity with the model that will make them employable and saleable. In each case, the activity of self-production is the key that unlocks the social world.

The specifically political scope of this power is excellently described by Naomi Klein throughout her book, *No Logo* (2000). Among other things we find there an account of the backdrop to her childhood, thronged with symbols, figures and images that were much more vivid and emotionally charged than the natural 'wilderness' her parents tried to get her to appreciate. And an account of food that came in 'shiny laminated boxes', that was much more appetizing than the organic produce she was supposed to eat.[16] The omnipresent advertising of the big corporations exerts a total stranglehold on public space, feeds the imagination with its fantastic narratives and creations, shapes taste and provides aesthetic norms. It invades classrooms and, with the complicity of teachers, provides subjects for students' essays. It colonizes the media, practising censorship on a part of the press and broadcasting. It appropriates cultural life, first by using artistic works to promote brands and then, reversing the procedure, by putting commercial brand names on presentations of art works. After using famous works to lend itself an aura of excellence, the brand name then lays claim to itself being the symbol and criterion of excellence. Everything the brand stamps its logo on is seen as excellent; and the logo will serve to promote the sale of anything whatever. It is the brand that gives the product its value—not the other way about.[17]

The direct function of advertising, concludes Robert Kurz, is not so much

> to get people to buy particular commodities, as to engender a consciousness that has internalized the form, meaning and specific aesthetic of 'advertising in general' and sees the world through its eyes [. . .] The shaping not just of wants and desires, but also of feelings, the stranglehold on the Unconscious, reveal the totalitarian character of capitalism most distinctly—and make the to-

talitarianism invisible, insofar as that stranglehold is successful.[18]

And, as Ben Bagdikian writes,

> Nothing in earlier history matches this corporate group's power to penetrate the social landscape [. . .] At issue is the possession of power to surround almost every man, woman and child [. . .] with controlled images and words, to socialize each new generation of Americans, to alter the political agenda of the country. And with that power comes the ability to exert influence that in many ways is greater than that of schools, religion, parents, and even government itself.[19]

In *No Logo*, Klein charts both the method and the extent of this stranglehold on public spaces and the resistance it encounters. The developing and intensifying conflict between the immaterial capital of corporations and the actors resisting it is, in many ways, a class struggle shifted on to a new terrain—that of the control of the public domain, of shared culture and collective goods. The resisters, organized at times on a large scale—or, rather, self-organized, at times locally and at others internationally through the Internet—are movements of school and university students, consumers and residents, all resolved to reconquer the public domain, reappropriate urban space and reclaim power over their environment, shared culture and daily lives.

> Thousands of groups today are all working against forces whose common thread is what might broadly be described as the privatization of every aspect of life, and the transformation of every activity and value into a commodity. We often speak of the privatization of education, of health care, of natural resources. But the process is much vaster. It includes the way powerful ideas are turned into advertising slogans and public streets into shopping malls; new generations being target-marketed at birth; schools being invaded by ads; basic human necessities like

water being sold as commodities; basic labour rights being rolled back; genes are patented and designer babies loom; seeds are genetically altered and bought; politicians are bought and altered [. . .]

[Throughout the world] activisits aren't waiting for the revolution, they are acting right now, where they live, where they study, where they work, where they farm [. . .] The fight against globalization has morphed into a struggle against corporatization and, for some, against capitalism itself [. . .] The real news out of Seattle is that organizers around the world are beginning to see their local and national struggles—for better funded public schools, against union-busting and casualization, for family farms, and against the widening gap between rich and poor—through a global lens [. . .] By focusing on corporations, organizers can demonstrate graphically how so many issues of social, ecological and economic justice are inter-connected.[20]

INTRINSIC VALUES AND WEALTH BEYOND MEASURE: EXTERNALITIES

I have put these two quotations from Bagdikian and Klein together because they cast a complementary light on two aspects of the same reality: capitalism's stranglehold on the last cost-free forms of wealth that it has not had to produce—and is, indeed, unsuited to producing—and the resistance that is being mounted against that stranglehold in all the fields in which it exerts itself. To prevent that resistance from crystallizing and spreading, capital has to get culture to internalize the domination capital exerts over it. It has to seize hold of the collective imagination, of shared norms and language. In the conflict that is looming, language is a central issue; on its mastery and control depends the possibility of conceiving and expressing resistance and the motivation for that resistance.

Words are not innocent when they 'naively' in-clude in the social relations of capital things which, just a few years ago, seemed necessarily to lie outside them. I am thinking of the burgeoning of different 'capitals' now present in dominant thinking: 'cultural capital', 'intellectual capital', 'educational capital', 'experiential capital', 'social capital', 'natural capital', 'symbolic capital', 'human capital' and, in particular, 'knowledge capital' or 'cognitive capital', this latter forming the basis of 'cognitive capitalism' or even of the—quite naturally, capitalist—'knowledge society', since '(formal) knowledge can be regarded as the new form of capital, through which the creative capacity of modern societies finds expression.'[21]

However, this 'new form of capital'—there are others—differs fundamentally from capital in the economic sense. It is not originally acquired or produced in order to become or remain the private property of its possessors. On the contrary, it becomes augmented with additional knowledge by being used and shared. It is not originally accumulated to serve as a means of production but to satisfy the need to know, the passion for knowledge—in other words, to get to the truth of that which is beyond appearance and use. It is not the product of surplus-value taken from the exploitation of labour. It is wealth and a source of wealth even when it gives rise to nothing that can be sold. It cannot grow by circulating in the value-form; on the contrary, it is by disseminating itself as a good accessible to all that it engenders additional knowledge.

In a word, its properties are precisely the opposite of the properties of capital in the economic sense. 'Knowledge capital' can function as capital only in the framework of—or, more precisely, *within*—capitalism when it is distorted by its association with traditional—financial and material—forms of capital. It is not capital in the usual sense and its primary intention is not to serve in the production of surplus-value or even value in the usual sense. It does not signify the coming of a hyper- or pan-capitalism, as its name might suggest but contains, rather, the seeds of a negation and transcendence of capitalism, commodity labour and commodity exchange.

To the confusion between the 'new forms of capital' and capital in the sense of political economy is
added the confusion between (exchange-)'value' in the
economic sense and the 'value' that has its source in
knowledge (and experience, culture, social relations,
etc.). 'Value will be determined only by humanity's
own continuous innovation and creation,' writes Antonio Negri,[22] and Bernard Paulré argues that 'Value is
mainly the product of change and innovation.'[23] More
fundamentally, Moulier-Boutang writes: 'Free activity
upstream and downstream from what is considered
by political economy (in all its various schools) as the
only activity deserving of remuneration is the main
source of value.'[24]

What does this mean? What 'value' is being re-
ferred to? Exchange-value, monetary and commercial,
which is the only value political economy knows (in all
its various schools)? The scarcity value of things that
are now a source of rent for their inventors? Or the
intrinsic value of what is intrinsically desirable and,
consequently, not exchangeable as a commodity for

other commodities. Isn't value employed also in the sense of 'wealth', as Marx does, for example, when he speaks of the production of 'use-values no longer measured by their exchange-value', in other words, of values that are no longer those commodities primarily made for sale—and hence can no longer be exchanged as a function of the market but, rather, like art works at a predetermined price that bears no relation to the cost of production.

All these questions are concertinaed in this remark by Rullani: 'In post-Fordism, knowledge produces value also because it generates meaning. The intrinsic value of what one does [. . .] becomes as important as the money value obtained on the market. For the musician who "sells" music, the result' is not measured only in money, but in 'the value of work that has a meaning in itself.'[25] Now, there is no relation of proportionality (and, even less, of equivalence) between these two 'values'. Money value in no sense reflects aesthetic value, which in no way reflects labour value. 'Intrinsic value' lies, by its very essence, outside the economy. The intrinsic values—aesthetic or ethical vital values in Max Scheler's sense (strength, agility, health, courage)—are neither comparable, exchangeable nor interchangeable. What Maurizio Lazzarato says of the 'truth value' of a book in his essay on Gabriel Tarde applies also to them: 'It is essentially intangible, inappropriable, unexchangeable, unconsumable and indivisible,' irrespective of the market value of the book as a material commodity. Aesthetic, cognitive or ideal creations are never really 'traded' or sold, since 'the person who hands them over does not lose them, does not deprive himself by socializing them,' and 'trading' in them benefits all parties concerned, who are enriched by their gifts. 'Consumption is not destructive, but creative of other knowledge. Consumption and production coincide in the consumption of knowledge' or of aesthetic or ideal creations.[26]

'The knowledge economy' thus contains, at heart, a negation of the capitalist commercial economy. By treating it as 'the new form of capitalism', its poten-

tial for negativity is concealed. Knowledge, inseparable from the capacity to know, is produced at the same
time as the knowing subject. It is a *truth-value* before it
is a *means of production*. More precisely, not all knowledge lends itself to serving as a means of production
and that which does so intentionally and from the outset is distinguished by its instrumental effectiveness,
not by the truth-value of its contents. This is to say
that not all knowledge is the same and capitalism retains and valorizes as a source of value only that
knowledge whose instrumental potentiality is clear or
predictable.

Following Lazzarato and Tarde, we should, then,
distinguish between truth-knowledge, beauty-knowl-
edge and wisdom-knowledge, on the one hand, and the
instrumental knowledge that can be 'capitalized' on the
other. Insofar as any form of knowledge, even the instrumental (i.e. the practico-technical), necessarily
contains an implicit relation to truth-knowledge and to
the capacity to know and learn, all knowledge, even the
technical, is not just a potential source of wealth and

meaning but also something valuable in itself. As a *source of wealth*, it is a 'productive force'; as *wealth*, it is a source of meaning and an end in itself. As productive force, it is labour-power—but *being put to work is neither the exclusive nor the prime destiny of knowledge.*

To treat *knowledge* as capital and as a means of production is, ultimately, to reduce the whole of human activity—all cognitive, aesthetic, relational and bodily capacities, etc.—to instrumental activities of production, that is to say, to capitalist productivism and its indifference to contents. The paradigm of production for production's sake and accumulation for accumulation's sake is simply extended from the field of commodities and capital to that of innovation and of knowledge-productive-of-productive-knowledge, regarded as an end in itself with no concern for the orientation and sense of that accumulation. It is from this angle that cognitive capitalism is an extension of capitalism while at the same time perverting the specificity of the social relations of knowledge.

The distinction between 'productive force' and 'means of production'—between 'wealth' and 'value'—appears essential, then, insofar as it marks the limits of instrumental reason and grounds the internal critique of cognitive capitalism, as it does of industrial capitalism. Like culture, wisdom, tacit knowledge, artistic, relational and cooperative capacities, etc., (formal) knowledge is both wealth *and* a source of wealth without either being or having a monetary market value. It is—like the other human capacities—a productive force *without being only that*, and without necessarily being a *means* of production. Like the other human capacities, like health, life and nature (which is also a productive force *without being only that*), it is part of that 'external' wealth or those 'externalities' which are indispensable to the system of commodity production but which that system is incapable of producing by its own logic and methods. Capital can exploit these riches by pillage and 'predation' in the same way as it exploits non-producible natural resources to derive (extractive, property or touristic) rents from them. I would like to see someone develop the anti-capitalist implications of Moulier-Boutang's argument on the crucial place occupied by 'predation on externalities' in the development of the economy.[27]

At the beginnings of British capitalism, these externalities were the common lands or 'commons', a collective good the inhabitants cultivated or used to graze their livestock, which the landowners appropriated by enclosing them and dividing them up (enclosures). In America, they were the empty spaces of the West. They included also, as they still do, the unpaid 'work of reproduction' performed by women to maintain the male labour force and carry out the primary socialization of children. Today, they include such 'collective goods of humanity' as biodiversity, genomes and living forms of practical knowledge currently being patented and privatized, and, lastly, the shared natural and urban spaces, landscapes, etc., that Klein speaks of. And also living knowledge and, more widely, the human capacities produced by and in cooperation, interaction, communication and affective relations. Cooperative activity expands the capacity to produce activity; it produces a total activity that exceeds the capacities of each and feeds back positively into those capacities. Positive externalities are the outcome of the positive feedback of synergies that develop outside the enterprise, before being harnessed and 'valorized' by that enterprise as 'human capital'.

The 'privatization of every aspect of life, and the transformation of every activity and value into a commodity' to which Klein refers are, in the end, 'predations on externalities' of the same kind as those highlighted by the theorists of 'cognitive capitalism'.

The potentially preponderant importance now accorded to externalities shows up the limits of the market economy and throws its categories into crisis. It brings out the fact that primary wealth, the potential source and precondition of all other forms, is not producible by any enterprise, accountable in any currency or exchangeable for any equivalent. It reveals that the visible—so-called formal—economy is merely a relatively small part of the total economy. Domination by the formal economy has rendered in-

visible the existence of a primary economy constituted of non-commodity activities, exchanges and relations by which are produced meaning, the capacity
for love, for cooperating, for feeling and for bonding
with others, for living in peace with one's body and
with nature.

It is in this *other economy* that individuals produce
themselves as humans, both mutually and individually,
and produce a shared culture. Recognition of the
primacy of external wealth over the economic system
requires the relationship between the production of
commodity 'value' and the production of 'intangible,
inappropriable, unexchangeable, unconsumable and
indivisible' wealth to be inverted—the former must
be subordinated to the latter.

Notes

1 Christian Marazzi, *La Place des chaussettes* (The Place of
   Socks; Paris: L'Éclat, 1997), p. 107. First published as *Il
   posto dei calzini* (Bellinzona: Casagrande, 1994).

2 William Thompson, *An Enquiry into the Principles of the Distribution of Wealth* (London: Longmans, 1824), p. 274. Cited in Karl Marx, *Capital: A Critique of Political Economy, Volume 1* (Harmondsworth: Penguin, 1976), pp. 482–83.

3 Adam Ferguson, *An Essay on the History of Civil Society* (Edinburgh: Printed for A. Millar and T. Cadell, London, and for A. Kincaid and J. Bell, 1767), p. 281. Cited in Marx, *Capital, Volume 1*, p. 484.

4 Marx, *Grundrisse*, pp. 693–95. [Translation modified. It should be said that this is a composite quotation assembled by Gorz and that the words quoted do not necessarily occur in this order in Marx's text.—Trans.]

5 See André Gorz, 'Technique, techniciens et lutte des classes' (Technology, Technicians and Class Struggle), in *Critique de la division du travail* (Critique of the Division of Labour; Paris: Le Seuil, 1972), pp. 249–87.

6 Enzo Rullani, 'Le capitalisme cognitif: du déjà vu?' (Cognitive Capitalism: Déjà Vu?) *Multitudes* 2 (May 2000).

7 Ibid.

8 Jeremy Rifkin, *The Age of Access: The New Culture of Hypercapitalism Where All of Life is a Paid-for Experience* (New York: Putnam, 2000).

9 Marazzi, *La Place des chaussettes*, p. 104.

10 It is clear, however, that only the 30 per cent who are relatively well-off can continue to pile up debt. 'The American miracle,' writes Edward Luttwak, 'produces many losers and few winners. 55 per cent of the active American population work as salesmen, waiters and waitresses, cleaners, domestic servants, gardeners, nannies and janitors, and half of them are in low-paid precarious employment, more than a quarter are "working poor", whose income is below the poverty line, even when they have two or three jobs.' Cf. *Turbocapitalism* (New York: Harper Collins, 1999). [The quotation from Luttwak does not actually appear to be from *Turbocapitalism*, but Gorz gives no source for it. The text is therefore a back-translation from the French.—Trans.]

11 In the plural economy project promoted by the *Transversales* journal (see Issue 003, 2002), consumption money, the idea of which was coined by Jacques Duboin in the early 1930s, is one of the four kinds of money. *Its aim is not to monetize reciprocal local trade or cooperative activities, but to ensure access for all to those things that can be produced only on the basis of a macrosocial division of labour or to those things that are producible without labour and hence are without monetary value.*

12 Cf. André Gorz, 'Living-Dead Capitalism' in *Paths to Paradise* (Malcolm Imrie trans.) (London: Pluto, 1985), pp. 35–9.

13 See ibid., p. 6.

14 Between 24 March and 14 April 2002, BBC2 broadcast a documentary of exceptional quality, Adam Curtis' *The Century of the Self*. In four one-hour episodes, it tells the history of the manipulation of the 'consumer' and, subsequently, of the citizen, through marketing and market-research techniques from 1920 to 2001.

15 Cf. André Gorz, *Critique of Economic Reason* (Gillian Handyside and Chris Turner trans.) (London: Verso, 1989), pp. 44–7.

16 Naomi Klein, *No Logo* (London: Flamingo, 2000), p. 144.

17 Ibid., pp. 27–61.

18 Robert Kurz, *Schwarzbuch des Kapitalismus* (The Black Book of Capitalism) (Frankfurt: Eichborn, 1999), p. 571.

19 Ben Bagdikian, *The Media Monopoly* (Boston: Beacon Press, 1997), p. ix. Cited in Rifkin, *The Age of Access*, p. 223.

20 Naomi Klein, 'Reclaiming the Commons', *New Left Review* 9 (May–June 2001): 81–5.

21 See Christian Azaïs, Antonella Corsani and Patrick Dieuaide (eds), *Vers un capitalisme cognitif* (Towards a Cognitive Capitalism; Paris: L'Harmattan, 2000), p. 10.

22 See Antonio Negri and Michael Hardt, *Empire* (Cambridge: Harvard University Press, 2000), p. 356.

23 Bernard Paulré, 'De la *new economy* au capitalisme cognitif' (From the 'New Economy' to Cognitive Capitalism), *Multitudes* 2 (May 2000).

24 Yann Moulier-Boutang, 'Richesse, propriété, liberté et revenu dans le capitalisme cognitif' (Wealth, Property, Freedom and Income in Cognitive Capitalism), *Multitudes* 5 (May 2001).

25 Enzo Rullani, 'Production de connaissance et valeur dans le postfordisme' (The Production of Knowledge and Value in Post-Fordism; interview with Antonella Corsani), *Multitudes* 2 (May 2000).

26 Maurizio Lazzarato, 'Travail et capital dans la production de connaissances: une lecture à travers l'oeuvre de Gabriel Tarde' (Labour and Capital in the Production of Knowledge: An Interpretation Based on the Work of Gabriel Tarde) in Azaïs et al. (eds.), *Vers un ca-*

pitalisme cognitif, pp. 159–60. See also Antonella Corsani, 'Éléments d'une rupture. L'hypothèse du capitalisme cognitif' (Elements of a Break. The Cognitive Capitalism Hypothesis), in ibid., p. 185; and Maurizio Lazzarato, *Puissances de l'invention* (Powers of Invention; Paris: Les Empêcheurs de penser en rond, 2000), pp. 164–74.

27 See Moulier-Boutang, 'La troisième transition du capitalisme', pp. 135ff.; 'Éclat d'économie et bruits de luttes' (Economic Lustre and Sounds of Struggle), *Multitudes* 2 (May 2000).

CHAPTER THREE

TOWARDS AN INTELLIGENT SOCIETY? . . .

REDEFINING WEALTH

'Cognitive capitalism' is the mode in which capitalism perpetuates itself when its categories have lost their relevance: when the production of wealth is no longer calculable or quantifiable in terms of 'value'; when the main productive force is no longer a rare resource or a privatizable means of production but a set of plentiful, inexhaustible forms of human knowledge, which, when used and shared, increase in scope and availability.

Though virtually outstripped by developments, capitalism perpetuates itself by employing a plentiful resource—human intelligence—to produce scarcity, including scarcity of intelligence. This production of scarcity in a situation of potential plenty consists in raising obstacles to the circulation and pooling of knowledge in its various forms. This is done, among other things, through the control and privatization of the means of communication and access, and through concentration on a very narrow stratum of competences that are allowed to function as 'cognitive capital'.

'Cognitive capitalism', which is a tissue of incoherences and contradictions that make it extremely unstable and vulnerable, is shot through with cultural conflicts and social antagonisms. And it is precisely because of its instability, incoherence, complex, unbalanced (class) structure and the narrowness of its social base that 'cognitive capitalism' contains within it the possibility of rapid development in opposing directions. It isn't a capitalism *in crisis*—it *is the crisis* of capitalism which is shaking society to its roots.

We have seen the economic symptoms of this crisis in the prolonged inflation of the stock-market bubble and its implosion after 2001. That bubble revealed the difficulty capitalism finds in transforming the essentially non-measurable, non-exchangeable value of 'immaterial capital' into (monetary) value, in making that function as capital and in making 'cognitive capitalism' function as a capitalism. The monetary equivalents of both assets and immaterial commodities no longer measure anything measurable. They reflect relations of force, not relations of equivalence.

Equally revealing of a deep-seated disturbance is the importance business consultancies now accord to positive externalities as sources of wealth. In an article that substantially confirms certain analyses made by Lazzarato, Moulier-Boutang and Negri and his colleagues, Hervé Sérieyx shows that, in order to master the complexity of their environments, companies have to depend on the proliferation of the activities of the members of their staff and on multilateral interactions among them, and not attempt to dominate them by seeking to measure their individual performance. Persons who cooperate, coordinate with, and adapt to, one another freely in a project they have defined between them will each tend to excel. Like a free-jazz combo, all will feel prompted by the others to develop their capacities, their receptiveness and their focus on results. The survival of the enterprise in a complex environment depends on this capacity for self-organization, on its ability to 'foster the development of collective and individual intelligence'.[1]

Clearly, the individual contributions to the collective result are thereby rendered unmeasurable. The notions of labour time and quantity of labour lose their relevance. The source of productivity lies in *an organization that promotes self-organization* and generates positive externalities—that is to say, a collective outcome that transcends the sum of individual contributions.

Just like the promoters of Free Software and Free Networks, Sérieyx is convinced that 'the learning organization' can and must be the paradigm for a different society, for a 'learning society, the rules of which—constitution, laws, principles of collective life—would be designed to enable each citizen to learn by doing and to enable the community, in action, to keep on increasing a better distributed "Gross National Happiness".'[2] What we have here is the blueprint for an *intelligent society* in which the full development of each person's abilities is everyone's aim.

Sérieyx's article is interesting not for the intrinsic novelty of its thinking but for the fact that that thinking is presented as arising from a concern for 'survival' and optimum efficiency. It suggests that, in the era of 'general intellect', economic rationality consists in subordinating economic rationality to criteria different from those that have defined and measured it hitherto. Optimum efficiency can no longer be obtained by pursuing maximum output of immediate labour, getting maximum performance out of each individual or by maximizing profit. It can no longer be got by making all factors of production measurable, in order to be able to maximize the output of each. Economic rationality is no longer what it was. It now demands that the usual criteria of output be subordinated to the criterion of human development and, hence, to a fundamentally different rationality.

In its development of the productive forces, capitalism has thus arrived at a boundary beyond which it can exploit its potentialities to the full only by transcending itself in the direction of a different economy. The potential agent of this transcendence is 'human capital' itself, insofar as it is tending to emancipate itself from capital. We shall see soon to what extent this tendency is manifesting itself. But we are aware, as Sérieyx writes, that 'there are few learning organizations.' For capital, the domination of labour-power has always been the condition of its utilization. It is better, from its standpoint, to give up on certain potential externalities than to give up dominating labour.

Once one grasps the crucial importance of resources like collective intelligence that have no equivalent, are not quantifiable or measurable and, hence, not exchangeable in the market, one arrives at another conception of wealth and the goals of human activity. One discovers that there is such a thing as intrinsic wealth and that it is currently being destroyed by an economy that knows no other values but those of the market. The economicization of all activities and all wealth becomes destructive of meaning, impoverishes social relations, degrades the urban milieu and the natural environment, generates negative externalities, the cost of which the system cannot and will not evaluate. The link between 'more' and 'better', between 'value' (in the economic sense) and 'wealth' is broken. We are living worse while spending more money, and we believe we have to earn more and more. Sérieyx alludes to this when he contrasts Gross National Happiness, which clearly has no exchange-value, to the Gross National Product, which measures exchange in terms of value. Wealth becomes a notion to be redefined and to be shifted out of the hegemonic ambit of economic categories.[3]

As starting point and basis for a redefinition, I
shall take this short passage from the *Grundrisse*, which
pops up, as though from a sudden burst of inspira-
tion, towards the end of an outline of the history of
economic systems:

> [W]hen the limited bourgeois form is stripped
> away, what is wealth other than the universal-
> ity of individual needs, capacities, pleasures,
> productive forces, etc., created through uni-
> versal exchange? The full development of
> human mastery over the forces of nature,
> those of so-called nature as well as of human-
> ity's own nature? The absolute working-out of
> his creative potentialities, with no presupposi-
> tion other than *the previous historic development,
> which makes this totality of development, i.e. the de-
> velopment of all human powers as such, the end in it-
> self, not as measured on a predetermined yardstick?*[4]

What is particularly interesting about this passage
is that the surpassing of capitalism is defined here as
a necessary surpassing of productivism. The economy

ceases to dominate society, human forces and capacities cease to be *means* for producing wealth—they are wealth itself.

The source of wealth is the activity that develops human capacities or, more specifically, the 'work' of self-production that 'individuals'—each and all, each in their multilateral dealings with all—carry out on themselves. The full development of human capacities and faculties is both the aim of activity and that activity itself—there is no separation between the aim and the ever incomplete pursuit of that aim.

A basic inversion takes place here—humanity is no longer in the service of the development of production but production in the service of human development, that is to say, of the production of self. The difference between producing and producing oneself tends to disappear. The work of production is carried out in the way that best serves 'the development of . . . [a] rich individuality which is as all-sided in its production as in its consumption and whose labour also therefore appears no longer as

labour, but as . . . [personal] activity itself.'[5] The elim-
ination of productivism ushers in a new relationship
to time, one's own body and Nature, which is reflected
in the 'capacity for pleasure' and the 'aptitude for
leisure' (*Mussefähigkeit*), for artistic activities and for
other non-instrumental activities.

THE DISSIDENTS OF DIGITAL CAPITALISM

A society in which the full development of each is the
common aim of all defines itself essentially as a 'society of culture' (*Kulturgesellschaft*) or, in other words,
as a society that sets as its central task—and assumes
as its chief value—culture in the sense of *Bildung*, in
the sense of cultivating our sensory, affective, expressive and bodily faculties; in the sense, as Méda writes,
of 'cultivating our minds, of constantly working-over,
deepening, moulding and shaping the dispositions
given to us, the individual and social heritage with
which we are endowed.'[6]

Once we have shown that such a redefinition of
wealth is what is haunting the crisis of the main cate-

gories of political economy—and, particularly, the crisis of the concepts of capital and value—then 'one
of the priorities,' writes Patrick Viveret, 'is to detect
the persons and groups with the cultural and spiritual
visions that play—or will play—a key role in ushering
in the idea that humanity has entered on a new era
and needs new conceptual, cultural and ethical frame-
works to accompany this great change.'[7] I suggested
earlier, with regard to Sérieyx's article, that the potential agent of the transcendence of capitalism (in the
direction of a different economy) was 'human capital' itself, insofar as it is tending to free itself from
capital. It is this trend that is most clearly highlighted
by the struggle being conducted, at the very heart of
capitalism's systems of power, by the architects of
Free Software and Free Networks. In their persons, at
least some of those who possess 'human capital' at its
highest technical level stand opposed to the privatization of the means of access to that 'common good
of humanity' that is knowledge in all its forms. This
is a social and cultural dissidence based overtly on a

different conception of the economy and society. And it has strategic import, given the importance of what the Americans call the 'knowledge class' for the development of society and its conflicts.

Peter Glotz has examined this question in a book whose eloquent title translates as *Accelerated Society: The Cultural Conflicts in Digital Capitalism*.[8] In it, he sketches out a class analysis on the basis of the American fiscal statistics and occupational classifications on which writers like Christopher Lasch, Robert Reich, along with Rifkin, have also drawn. The data cited by these authors show that power and wealth have never before been concentrated in so few hands. Less than 0.5 per cent of the American population (843,000 families) hold 56.2 per cent of the tangible means of production and 37.4 per cent of financial assets. Beneath this stratum of the super-rich, we find a class of new professionals, including, among others, the 'symbolic analysts' (3.8 million people or 4 per cent of the working population) who manage the high-tech information economy. The income of this 4 per cent is equal to that of the 51 per cent (49.2 million) workers at the bottom of the income pyramid. To this knowledge elite, we should also add the 16 per cent who are members of the intellectual professions. Thus the members of the 'knowledge class' represent 20 per cent of the working population and share between them half of the GDP.

We should not, however, conclude, argues Glotz, that these 20 per cent represent the totality of the workers in the immaterial economy or—and this amounts to the same—that all the workers in the immaterial economy are in the most affluent one-fifth of the population. We should be aware that more than 90 per cent of the fruits of 15 years of economic growth have been monopolized by the richest 5 per cent of the population and, what is more, 60 per cent have been taken by the richest 1 per cent. We should be aware, too, that the incomes of 80 per cent of the population have fallen; there has been a meltdown of the 'middle classes'; and the polarization of society has given rise to a new post-industrial proletariat which, by Glotz's estimation, forms around one-third of the population. Furthermore, this proletariat, 'unlike that of industrial societies', includes a high proportion of dissidents with higher education qualifications who have a critical attitude towards 'digital capitalism' and its cult of 'more and faster'. According to a survey by the *Wall Street Journal*, 'more than 35 per cent of recent graduates have been forced to take jobs that don't require a college degree [. . .] The job market for college graduates is now the poorest since World War II.'[9]

The interesting new development is that a number of high-level IT specialists form part of this post-industrial neo-proletariat in a common rejection of the 'nanosecond culture', as Glotz calls it—that is to say, the culture of ever-increasing speed. The ruling class (the 0.5 per cent) have probably succeeded in co-opting the techno-scientific elites that capitalism needs. But the members of that select band, while committing themselves fully to their work, do not all wish to devote the entirety of their lives to it. A high proportion of IT high-flyers know that once they are past 30 or 35, they are under threat of burnout or, in other words, of a kind of mental fatigue which can make work whose difficulty initially stimulated their creativity seem insipid, wearisome and meaningless. During their years of intense activity, many are preparing to sell off the companies they have created, live from their investments and work only as consultants two days a week, often on a charitable basis. Their relations with their peers generally remain informal and relaxed at the personal level, even when they are intensely competitive professionally.

The boundary between the digitial elite and the digital proletariat remains especially porous. Within a single stratum of professionals, one finds both young retired millionnaires, young graduates who refuse to sacrifice everything for their careers and self-entrepreneurs who work only part time because they don't have many clients or are unwilling to 'fight dirty' to gain a foothold in the marketplace. As Glotz observes:

The really new element is that a growing number of people are joining the neoproletariat from choice, because they reject the nanosecond culture. More and more young people are tending to refuse to climb the greasy pole, to prefer more free time to more money, to transform their full-time employment into working shorter hours and to dispense with the work ethic [. . .] They will take as their model the teacher who reduces his working hours by one third in the conviction that his commitment to his children and his household has a hundred times more value than the work of the hypercompetitive programmer who gives his all for Microsoft, Java-Script or hypertext.

[. . .]

The more digital capitalism extends its hold over our lives, the greater will be the number of downshifters [. . .] They will give rise to a new conception of the world. The struggle that will pit the digital proletariat against the digital elite will not be around technocratic and economic issues but, in the main, around two conceptions of life rooted in principles and passions. The entire social ethic of modern capitalism is in question.[10]

I have quoted Glotz at considerable length here because I find in the work of this acute witness to his age the idea of the 'postindustrial neoproletariat', which I regarded in 1980 as the main future agent of an anti-productivist, anti-statist cultural shift.[11] What has changed since that date is that, with the development of the Web and the Free Software movement, this neoproletariat has, the world over, become the site towards which all radical opposition to globalized, financialized capitalism has converged—or from which it has emanated.

Software is, in fact, both a means of network creation and a means of transmission, communication, pooling of resources, exchange and production. Capital's command authority is no longer embedded in and guaranteed by the materiality and the private ownership of one of the main means of production and exchange. Not only does software lend itself to collective appropriation, to shared usage and to being made freely available to all, but it also virtually demands these things, because they increase its effectiveness and usefulness. The virtual, potentially universal community of users and producers of Free Software and Networks sets up social relations that represent the beginnings of a practical negation of capitalist social relations.

Stefan Merten, the founder of the Oekonux website, which explores the possibilities of 'a different economy and society, beyond work, money and exchange', points out that 'most Free Software producers' are solely motivated by their desire for personal self-unfolding [*Selbstentfaltung*]: 'The self-unfolding of the single person is present in the process of production.'[12]

The 'developer' is driven solely by 'the desire to communicate, act together, socialize, and differentiate herself not by the exchange of services but by congenial relations,' writes Lazzarato.[13] For hackers like Linus Torvalds—one of the leading pioneers of Free Software—explains Pekka Himanen, the basic organizing factor isn't money or work but the passion and the desire to create something that gives them social standing with others—in other words, something that gains them recognition from their peers. The hacker's activity is based on an ethics of voluntary cooperation, in which each person coordinates freely with others and vies with them only over the quality and value of what they can 'bring to the pot'. Nothing is produced for commodity exchange. Exchange-value never comes into the calculations; all that counts is use-value which is, by its nature, unmeasurable. There is no quid pro quo and 'no need for reciprocity: you simply take what you need and you provide what you like,'[14] says Merten. Unlike the 'digital aristocracy', the hacker community rejects any productivist principle: 'The different sequences of life—work, family, friends, hobbies—are combined in such a way that work never occupies the centre . . . It leaves pride of place to entertainment and individual creativity' (Himanen).

In the ethic and aesthetic of the hackers we find, then, the *practical implementation* of the definition essayed by Marx in the passage quoted earlier, of wealth with its 'bourgeois form [. . .] stripped away'. And, in particular, we find work made consonant with 'personal activity'—contributing to full self-development on the same footing as the culture of free time—and the replacement, to the greatest possible degree, of commodity relations based on exchange-value by 'agreement on what should be produced, and how and to what end [. . .] The Linux community is the blueprint for a new organization of work and management, which could lead to a new economy.'[15] 'It is not inconceivable that it could define work in the twenty-first century as industrial organization defined it in the twentieth.'[16]

All this might well seem risible if we were talking about a utopian 'vision'. But we are talking about a *practice* which, setting out from a 'learning (self-)orga-

nization' inherent in Free Software, is developing con-
sciously within capitalism against capitalism, like a 'really existing anarcho-communism', to use Richard
Barbrook's phrase;[17] about a practice which intends to
wrangle with capital over the strategically highly sen-
sitive terrain of the production, orientation, division
and ownership of knowledge.

'ANOTHER WORLD IS POSSIBLE'

I shall come back at greater length to the question of
the nature, division and orientation of knowledge. For
the moment, the important thing is that the activist
communities in the Free Software movement are an
integral part of direct action networks whose aim is to
demonstrate that a different world and a different life
are possible. 'The really existing anarcho-communism'
of the 'Free' movement is a practice, not a programme. *The practice is the programme.* The goal is not
transcendent to the action. The other components of
the movement against the 'commodification of the
world' conduct themselves according to this same

principle: their aim is to 'change the world without taking power'[18] by hollowing out and delegitimizing the power of the institutions and authorities that hold it, by wresting ever larger spaces of autonomy from the planetary grip of capital and (re)appropriating the things capital has taken from people. It is as though the Free Software movement and other movements such as 'Reclaim the Streets', 'Ya Basta!', 'People's Global Action', 'Un autre monde est possible', 'Via campesina' or the 'Zapatista Army of National Liberation' (which has never fired a shot in anger but has succeeded in uniting dozens of other movements around a common charter) are the components of a single movement that is constantly differentiating and re-forming, for which the Free Networks could be said to be the common matrix—a non-hierarchical structure in centreless horizontal networks ceaselessly producing and organizing themselves, based on the principle of 'democracy by consensus' in which any proposal is considered, debated, enhanced and further elaborated by everyone's contributions.

There will be no revolution through the overthrow of the system by external forces. The negation of the system spreads within the system itself by the alternative practices, to which it gives rise. The most dangerously virulent of these for the system are the ones it cannot do without. As Pascal Jollivet writes, commenting on Himanen's *The Hacker Ethic*:

> Capitalism can function only if there are spheres of activity in which human behaviour is freed from capitalist logic [. . .] This paradox is at the heart of our times [. . .] The dilemma that faces companies in the new information economy is that capitalist success is possible only if communism continues to prevail among most researchers.[19]

The 'communism of researchers' or the anarcho-communism of the Free Networks can clearly be prefigurations of another possible world only if they spread into the social body as a whole and are catalysts to its re-formation. A global change seems possible only if it is carried forward by a coalition of a certain

type. Revolutions are made—when they are made—
by an alliance between the most oppressed and those
most aware of their own and other people's alienation.
It is this alliance that is on the cards in the many-sided
movement for a 'different world', a different sort of
globalization. Its different components are driven by
a plethora of academics, economists, writers, artists
and scientists, linked with and radicalized by opposi-
tional trade-unionists, post-industrial neo-proletarians,
cultural minorities, landless peasants and unemployed
and insecurely employed people. 'The more digital
capitalism extends its grip on our lives, the greater will
be the number of dissidents,' wrote Glotz. 'A new
worldview will emerge from them.'[20] The stakes in the
conflict were, in his view, essentially cultural, whereas
in reality, the cultural conflict masks some profoundly
political issues. Experimentation with other ways of
life and other social relations in the interstices of a
society that is falling apart attacks the control capital
exerts on minds and bodies and delegitimates it. The
constraints and values of capitalist society are no

longer perceived as natural, and this liberates the powers of imagination and desire.

THE ARGUMENTS FOR A BASIC INCOME

It is from this angle, first, that we should assess the
idea of a universal, unconditional, guaranteed social
income. The idea had been doing the rounds for a
long time, but it was with the strikes and demonstra-
tions of 1995 and 1997 that it became a plausible
demand in France and, by contagion, in other countries. Its heuristic value is enormous (I shall come back
to this), as is its capacity to unite a wide range of
social forces in an anti-capitalist perspective. As Reiner
Hartel writes,

> What is so delightful and attractive about the
> call for a basic income is that it enables al-
> liances to be formed that run from quasi-
> institutional associations for environmental
> and nature conservancy, trade unions, the
> women's movement and the representatives
> of charitable associations to workers' oppo-

sition groups in factories, committees of the unemployed, welfare claimants and immigrant groups. This kind of alliance of 'progressive' social forces is precisely what makes it possible to conceive a political perspective transcending capitalism.[21]

But to open up a perspective of this kind, the demand must involve, first and foremost, the guarantee of a *sufficient* income. The income must be sufficient, because any guarantee of an insufficient income functions as a disguised subsidy to employers—it justifies them in creating, and encourages them to create, jobs with inadequate wages and shameful working conditions. And the demand for an unconditionally guaranteed sufficient income must, above all, signify from the outset that dependent work is no longer the only way of creating wealth or the only type of activity whose social value is to be acknowledged. The guarantee of a sufficient income must mark the growing—and potentially preponderant—importance of that other economy which creates intrinsic wealth that is neither measurable nor exchangeable. It must mark the break between the creation of wealth and the creation of value. It must bring out the fact that 'unemployment' means neither being socially inactive nor socially useless, but merely being useless in the *direct* valorization of capital.

The collective realization, propagated by movements and unions of the unemployed and the insecurely employed, that 'we are all potentially unemployed or casual/temporary workers' does not simply mean that we all need to be protected against casualization and interruptions of the wage-relation; it means also that *we all have a right to a social existence that doe not consist exclusively in that relation* and does not coincide with it; that we all contribute to the productivity of the economy unseen and indirectly, including through interruptions of, and discontinuities in, our employment. The social wealth produced is a collective good and the contribution of each person to its creation has never been measurable—and is so less than ever today; and the right to an—unconditional, universal—sufficient income amounts, ultimately, to pooling part of what is produced in common, knowingly or otherwise.

When an increasing proportion of 'labour-power' is no longer necessary or useful for the production of 'value', human activity can and must be able to flourish outside of capitalist relations—and against those relations—in the creation of intrinsic values and non-convertible wealth. The guaranteed sufficient income is a condition for this flourishing. We find confirmation of it in documents produced by the anti-unemployment network, AC! (Agir contre le chômage et la précarité), which display something like an extension of the 'hacker ethic': 'For most [unemployed people]', says Laurent Guilloteau, for example, 'it isn't a question of defending an illusory return to full employment, but of inventing and trialling a full employment of life.'[22] A document produced by the income commission of AC! states that,

> In our view, the basic guaranteed income isn't charity. It isn't payment for inactivity

which would entail an obligation to 'do something' [the implication being to do 'work']. In our view, the guaranteed income is a right. If we claim that right, this is because we play a part, one way or another, in the production of social wealth—or could play a part in it if we had the necessary means [. . .] We produce social wealth that is unremunerated [. . .] consisting in different forms of collective self-organization, of help and mutual assistance systems that help us to overcome everyday problems, to trade knowledge, and to take initiatives that enable us to escape poverty and boredom [. . .] *we want to acquire for ourselves the means to develop much more enriching activities than those we are confined to currently.*[23]

This text demonstrates an interesting slide from the economic justification of the guaranteed income to its non-economic—political—one. Initially, it bases the right to a guaranteed income on the production by the unemployed of 'unremunerated social wealth'. Should we, then, regard the guaranteed income as the 'payment' for a productive activity? The idea is abandoned almost as soon as it is suggested—the social wealth produced is the social bond in different forms, or, in other words, an intrinsic form of wealth. Now, if we pay people *because* they produce the social bond, we make the production of the social bond the *condition* for the guaranteed income. Not only does that income cease to be unconditional but also the use made of it by its recipients will be prescribed administratively, or, at least, monitored. We then fall back into the scenario of 'citizen activities', remunerated by a 'citizenship wage'.

The idea of a guaranteed income linked to 'the obligation to do something' and remunerating that something is thus explicitly rejected. The unconditionally guaranteed basic income is seen as one of the means of developing infinitely 'more enriching activities', activities that *are* forms of creation of a wealth that is neither measurable nor exchangeable by any 'predetermined yardstick'. We find here once again the break between wealth with 'its bourgeois form [. . .] stripped away' and value in the economic sense. We find also the same inversion of the relation between activity and income as in the Free Software movement: income is no longer conceived as payment or reward for wealth-creation; it is that which is to make possible engagement in activities that *are* wealth and are an end in and for themselves, the production of which *is* the product. It is that which is to enable 'creators to create, inventors to invent, and the multitude of actors who can cooperate without need either of companies, overseers or employers to invent society and create social bonds in the form of networks of free cooperation.'[24]

In short, the guaranteed income should make possible all those activities that take place outside of markets, accounting and prescribed norms and which *are* not themselves—and do not *produce* anything—exchangeable for anything else, or anything measurable or convertible into its monetary equivalent. This is why the principle of unconditionality is important—it has to remove the intrinsic value of unmeasurable activities from any social prescription and predefinition. It has to prevent these activities from being regarded institutionally as preconditions for the right to the basic income and thus being transformed into *means* of earning one's living. It has to prevent voluntary work from becoming compulsory for the unemployed. It has to see to it that 'the absolute working-out of [. . .] creative potentialities' becomes 'the end in itself, not as measured on a predetermined yardstick'.[25] And that this is pursued *because people want to do so*, not as a form of self-production under constraint, dictated by an imperative of employability.

Notes

1 Hervé Sérieyx, 'Organisation apprenante et complexité' (Learning Organization and Complexity), *Transversales* 002 (Summer 2002).

2 Ibid.

3 The need for this redefinition is at the heart of the 1996 Report of the UNDP, of the work of Amartya Sen, of

Méda's *Qu'est-ce que la richesse?* and, particularly, of Patrick Viveret's report, *Reconsidérer la richesse* (Reconsidering Wealth; Paris: La Documentation française, 2001) and of the special issue of *Transversales* 70 (August 2001). In continuance of the themes of the Viveret report, see Guy Roustang, *Démocratie: le risque du marché* (Democracy: The Market Risk; Paris: Desclée de Brouwer, 2002), pp. 158–68.

4 Marx, *Grundrisse*, p. 488. Emphasis mine [A.G.]. [Marx himself underlines the word 'predetermined'.—Trans.]

5 Ibid., p. 325.

6 Méda, *Qu'est-ce que la richesse?*, p. 325.

7 Patrick Viveret, 'L'humanité est-elle un "bien" pour elle-même?' (Is Humanity a 'Good' for Itself?), *Transversales* 66 (March 2001); and 'Reconsidérer la richesse (suite)' (Reconsidering Wealth (Continued)), *Partage* 158 (May 2002).

8 Peter Glotz, *Die beschleunigte Gesellschaft. Kulturkämpfe im digitalen Kapitalismus* (The Accelerated Society. Cultural Battles in Digital Capitalism; Munich: Kindler, 1999).

9 Jeremy Rifkin, *The End of Work* (New York: G. P. Putnam's Sons, 1995), p. 172.

10 Glotz, *Die beschleunigte Gesellschaft*, pp. 127–8.

11 See André Gorz, *Farewell to the Working Class: An Essay on Post-Industrial Socialism* (London: Pluto Press, 1982).

12 Stefan Merten, interviewed in French by Joanne Richardson, in Joanne Richardson (ed.), *Anarchitexts: Voices from the Global Digital Resistance* (New York: Autonomedia, 2005), p. 317. First published as 'Logiciel libre et éthique du développement de soi. Entretien avec Joanne Richardson', *Multitudes* 8 (March–April 2002).

13 Lazzarato, 'Travail et capital dans la production de connaissances', pp. 159–60.

14 Merten, in *Anarchitexts*, p. 319.

15 Walter Göhr, 'Auf dem Weg zum Nintendo-Sozialismus?, *Express* (December 2000). *Express* is the monthly magazine of the German trade union opposition.

16 T. W. Malone and R. J. Laubacher, 'The Dawn of the E-lance Economy', *Harvard Business Review* 76(5) (September–October 1998).

17 Richard Barbrook, 'The High-Tech Gift Economy', *First Monday* 3(12) (December 1998).

18 *Change the World Without Taking Power* is a book by John Holloway (London: Pluto Press, 2002) which does not quite meet the expectations evoked by its title. By con-

trast, Miguel Bensayag and Diego Sztulwark's book *Du contre-pouvoir* (Of Counter-power; Paris: La Découverte, 2001) is entirely consonant with Holloway's title.

19 Pascal Jollivet, 'L'éthique hacker de Pekka Himanen' (The Hacker Ethic of Pekka Himanen), *Multitudes* 8 (March–April 2002).

20 Glotz, *Die beschleunigte Gesellschaft*, p. 128.

21 Reiner Hartel, 'Exit to Paradise? Die strömende Linke und das Existenzgeld', *Express* 4 (1999).

22 See the interview with Laurent Guilloteau by Moulier-Boutang, 'AC!', *Futur antérieur* 43(3) (1997–98).

23 AC! Income Commission, 24 October 1998. Emphasis mine [A.G.].

24 Yann Moulier-Boutang, 'Propriété, liberté et revenu dans le "capitalisme cognitif"' (Property, Freedom and Income in 'Cognitive Capitalism'), *Multitudes* 5 (May 2001).

25 Marx, *Grundrisse*, p. 488.

CHAPTER FOUR

. . . OR TOWARDS A POST-HUMAN CIVILIZATION?

FORMAL VERSUS EXPERIENTIAL KNOWLEDGE, SCIENCE VERSUS THE WORLD OF THE SENSES: ADVANCES IN DEHUMANIZATION

Intelligence is a set of faculties indissociable from, and irreducible to, one another: the faculties of learning, judging, analysing, reasoning, anticipating, memorizing, calculating, interpreting, understanding, imagining, dealing with the unforeseen . . . It develops and assumes meaning only if the implementation of these faculties is required by the pursuit of a goal: by a plan, desire or need. It is inseparable from the capacity to deal with the solicitations, resistances or threats from the human environment by developing skills, bodily knowledge, curiosities and sensibilities that disclose the physical world, organize and differentiate its spatiality, temporality and the inexhaustible diversity of its sensory and formal qualities. That intelligence is inseparable, too, from the capacity to confront and communicate with others and to understand their intentions and feelings intuitively. Psychology has, in the end, demonstrated the obvious intuition that intelligence is inseparable from affective life, that is to say, from the feelings and emotions, needs and desires, fears, hopes or expectations of subjects. In the absence of these, the capacities to judge, anticipate, order or interpret are missing; there remain only the capacities to analyse, calculate and memorize—in short, only machine intelligence.

The fact that the civilization that is currently emerging presents or represents itself as a 'knowledge society' tells us a great deal about that civilization's dearth of meaning. Formal knowledge does not, in fact, necessarily imply intelligence—it is a much poorer thing. It is unaware of the importance—essential from the political standpoint—of the question a society needs to ask itself: what is and what is not of the order of knowledge? What is it to know and what do we wish or need to know?

Whereas the concept of intelligence covers the whole range of human faculties and may, as a consequence, serve as the basis for a conception of society as a society of culture, the concept of knowledge excludes this possibility. We have to go back here, once again, over the fundamental difference between formal and experiential knowing.

Formal knowledge is always, by definition, knowing an object—material or otherwise, real or not—as object existing in itself outside me, distinct from me and endowed with autonomy (*Selbstständigkeit* in the vocabulary of phenomenology). The known in this case is held to be known only if it is posited as an object whose existence owes nothing to me. It does not depend on me. I am not responsible for it.

The object is known in this sense only if its determinations identify any object that corresponds to them as the *same* object. This identification of an object by its determinations is clearly an abstract social construct. Science knows only such things of nature as it is able to grasp by dint of the principles and laws in terms of which it approaches it. Science forces nature, said Immanuel Kant, to answer the questions 'that Reason puts to it' and can learn from it only what its—science's—principles prepare it to look for. The determinations by which the object of (formal) knowledge is identified are, then, culturally and socially qualified. They confer on the object an identity that does not have the self-evidence of a lived reality. Formal knowledge is the result of a social process of learning insofar as it is, first and foremost, knowledge of the socially constituted determinations that will serve to ground a socially validated intellection of the real. It is the knowledge of the determinations valid in a given society and at a given time that is taught by educational institutions, whereas intuitive knowledge of the tangible reality of things themselves is acquired mainly through experience outside the education system and is, at least in part, censured or invalidated by that system, though it may conceivably find expression at the artistic level.

Our primary original relation to the world is not formal knowledge—it is intuitive, precognitive knowledge. We originally learn about the world by experience; we get to know it in its tangible reality and 'understand' it through our bodies; we unfold it, inform it and shape it by the exercise of our sensory faculties which are in turn 'shaped' by it. We get to know the world through our bodies, and to know our body through the actions by which it unfolds the world by unfolding itself in the world. It is this 'tangible world', known at the corporeal level and 'experienced' by the body which, as Edmund Husserl noted as early as 1906, 'is the only real world, the only world really perceived as existing, the only world of which we have—and can have—experience: our daily lifeworld'.[1]

Without this precognitive knowledge, nothing would be understandable, intelligible or meaningful to us. It is 'the ground of our certainties,' writes Husserl, the reservoir of facts on which our existence is built. It encompasses all the things we know and can do without ever having thematized them as formal knowledge—for example, the ability to walk, find our way around, speak, handle objects or understand the metalanguage of facial expressions and vocal intonations. We learned the language of the social lifeworld and how to deal with its objects by our usage of them. The range of our precognitive, informal knowledge represents something like the weft of our consciousness, the basis on which the sensory, affective and intellectual development of our person will be built— or for lack of which it will not.

The quality of cultures and civilizations depends on the dynamic equilibrium they are able to create between intuitive knowledge of the lifeworld and the development of formal knowledge. It depends on the synergy and positive feedback set up between the development of these two forms of knowledge. It depends on the ability that the development of formal knowledge will have to improve the quality of the life-world, the so-called quality of life. It depends on a social and natural environment that helps our faculties to flourish by the wealth of its forms, colours, sounds and materials, by its spatial organization, by the design of its habitations and tools, by the ease and multilaterality of communication and intercourse and by the modes of cooperation.

Does formal knowledge, which enables us to conceive things that cannot be intuitively understood, complement, correct and extend lived experiential knowledge? Does it extend its scope and horizon? Does it seek to be accessible to, and assimilable by, everyone? Does its development—the development of the sciences—allow itself to be guided and oriented by needs, desires and aspirations that come from the lifeworld? Is it articulated with the forms of informal knowledge with an eye to synergy or does it invalidate those forms by claiming a monopoly of true knowledge for science?

These questions are the founding themes of the cultural, social and political critique that lies at the origin of the Green movement. I have shown elsewhere that this movement did not arise out of a concern for the 'defence of nature' but out of a resistance to the private appropriation and the destruction of that common good *par excellence* that is the lifeworld.[2] This increasingly well-organized resistance stood out against the megatechnologies and against speculation on land prices; against the administrations that were depriving residents of their environment by chemical or noise pollution, by concreting over the land or by restricting access to free natural resources such as light, air, water, silence, space and vegetation. These acts of resistance and protest that were essentially cultural and local in appearance rapidly became politicized in the 1970s after, first, a group of British scientists, then shortly afterwards an American team commissioned by the Club of Rome had demonstrated that the type of growth of the industrial economies was destroying the natural foundations of life on earth and leading us to live increasingly badly at increasingly high cost.

The linkage between 'more' and 'better' was broken. The divorce between 'value' and 'wealth' that we examined in the preceding chapter now appears linked to the divorce between formal knowledge and informal lived knowledge. Megatechnological machines, which are supposed to control nature and bring it under human mastery, enslave human beings to the instruments of that mastery. It is the technoscientific megamachine that exercises agency, that megamachine which has abolished nature in order to dominate it and which forces humanity to serve that domination.

The development of technoscientific knowledge, crystallized in the machineries of capital, has not engendered a society of intelligence but, as Miguel Bensayag and Diego Sztulwark put it, a society of ignorance.[3] The great majority of people *know* more and more things, but have less and less *know-how* and *understanding*. Fragments of specialized knowledge are learned by specialists who know nothing of the context, scope and meaning and, above all, 'the independent combinatory that guides technology'.[4] Shared, accepted facts and intuitive knowledge are disqualified by a host of professional 'experts' who claim a monopoly of true knowledge. Illich dubbed those professions that set the seal on individuals' inability to take charge of their own lives in an incomprehensible world the 'disabling professions'.

Technoscience has produced a world that overwhelms, frustrates and violates the human body by the actions it demands of it and the accelerated and intensified reactions it prompts from it. The contradiction between bodily needs and knowledge, on the one hand, and the 'needs' of the techno-economic megamachine, on the other, has become pathogenic. Human bodies, writes Finn Bowring, have become:

> [. . .] obstacles [. . .] to the reproduction of machines. As George Dyson candidly describes it, humans have today become 'bottlenecks' in the circulation and processing of

149

knowledge and information: [. . .] 'We are now the bottleneck—able to absorb a limited amount of information, while producing even less, from the point of view of machines.'[5]

Human beings are 'obsolete'. They have to be equipped with chemical aids to 'tranquilize' their nervous systems, stressed as these are by the violations they have to suffer, and with electronic aids to increase their brain capacity. Science and capital have joined forces in this common undertaking, even though their goals are not identical. Only ecology, in the broad sense, is trying to develop a science in the service of the full flourishing of life and of an environment that makes such a flourishing possible and stimulates it. But we remember the manifesto in which some 40 famous scientists accused ecology of being an anti-science. This is because it operates, in its ecosophical extensions, on the basis of a holistic approach to complex systems. It is alone in attempting to understand life, not in order to dominate it but to treat it

considerately. It is alone, in this concern, in seeing itself as a component of culture, integrated and assimilated into experiential knowledge, illuminating the
quest for wisdom and the good life.[6]

SCIENCE AND THE HATRED OF THE BODY

The divorce between formal and experiential knowledge, between science and the lifeworld, has its source
in the 'mathematization of nature'. Husserl was the
first to demonstrate this in 1936 in *The Crisis of European Sciences and Transcendental Phenomenonology*.[7] Mathematization, better than any other technique, makes
it possible to render knowledge radically independent
of the experience of the world as perceived by the
senses. Through mathematization, the intellect provides itself with the means to abstract itself from the
obvious findings of lived experience. It forces itself to
confine its approach to rigorously law-governed operations and strictly defined laws. It frees thought from
the 'prison of the body', as René Descartes put it, a
formula since taken up in many variants down to our

own day, including the 'disembodied thought' of the pioneers of artificial intelligence.

But thought 'freed from the body' emancipates itself from that body by confining itself in the even more restrictive limits of an immaterial prison which, like a corset, forces it—and enables it—to function in a machine-like way, by 'bracketing out' (*ausschalten*), as Husserl puts it, all the ways of thinking and self-evident facts that are not indispensable to the technique of calculation, including, of course, the needs, desires, pleasures, pains, fears or hopes that form the perpetually rewoven fabric of consciousness. The intellect detached from affective life in this way, whose only intention is to function in accordance with the laws and rules of calculation—regarded as the laws and rules of thought freed from irrationality—then discovers layers of reality inaccessible to experience and to other modes of thinking. It makes the astonishing discovery that the laws that are the specific laws of the intellect freed from the gravitational realities of the body, are also the laws that govern the universe.

This is a discovery expressed even in their day by Johannes Kepler and Galileo Galilei, Gottfried Leibniz and René Descartes. The former two were convinced that the mathematical laws by which they had managed to account for the movements of the heavenly bodies were the language in which God had created . the universe. In 1854, George Boole demonstrated this decisively for the first time: the laws of thought were mathematical in essence; they were of the same nature as the laws of the universe. In other words, God had worked in the same language as the mathematicians. Hence the following conclusion: mathematical thought can generate systems that function according to laws; it can embody itself in *thinking machines* whereby what is specifically divine in man will surpass itself in the direction of new and higher forms of life.[8]

A hundred years later in 1956, Allen Newell and Herbert Simon provided the first practical confirmation of Boole's prediction—they designed a computer that demonstrated a theorem from Bertrand Russell and Alfred North Whitehead's *Principia Mathematica*, which, in the eyes of the pioneers of artificial intelligence, proved that man can create machines that operate in the same way as his mind and that, as Alan Turing would hint in 1963, 'the transfer of the souls of men [. . .] to their machines' might be envisaged.[9]

But all this can also be formulated in the opposite way, by saying not that the mind can beget machines that function as it does but, rather, that the machine-thinking, by which the mathematizing mind posits the real as pure exteriority, can beget the machinic exteriority of that thinking. Instead of begetting 'spiritual machines'[10] that will be the triumph of the mind in its most specifically divine form, mathematizing thinking begets the triumph of machines over minds that have chosen to function as machines.

Underlying the theories and achievements of artificial intelligence, there is, then, the conviction that the 'mind' is essentially 'thought', that thought is mathematical in its essence and that it matches up to its 'divine' essence only if it detaches itself from the body and frees itself from the 'passions', feelings and sensations that are essentially corporeal. Thought disembodied in this way would, it is supposed, be capable of a knowledge that surpasses what our experience of the physical world reveals to us. It would abolish the finitude arising from the natural factuality of life, from our inhering bodily in nature. It would be protected from errors and illusions by the fact that, operating in the knowledge of its own laws, it would absolve us from fuelling the operations of our intellects with our subjectivity. It would no longer have to assume responsibility or be answerable for itself. It would no longer be motivated by any determinate interest or goal. It would pursue knowledge for its own sake and regard indifference to contents, interests and passions as the condition of access to truth.

Consequently, it is no longer a question of transforming the world or dominating it, any more than it is a question for 'man' of producing himself for one determinate existence rather than another. It is a question, to borrow Paul Valéry's expression, of acceding to 'the supreme poverty of power without a purpose',[11] which regards any determinate existence as a 'downfall' [*déchéance*[12]].

Science is the only enterprise that has as its explicit object to free the 'mind' from its factuality and to be the equal of God. The rejection of bodily existence, finitude and death expresses the project of being self-grounding—of being *ens causa sui*—through a contemptuous hatred of nature and the naturalness of life; through a hatred of being born of woman and of having been born in a woman's body from the encounter of a sperm and an ovum. This hatred of the natural factuality of life and, as a result, of motherhood, has found a particularly forthright outlet in the efforts deployed by 'science' to substitute an artificial womb for the female uterus. The pretext invoked for achieving 'ectogenesis' is the concern to 'liberate woman from the servitudes of pregnancy'. But this concern soon reveals itself to be the transparent disguise for another—to effect a techno-scientific rationalization of human reproduction.

Joseph Fletcher, a Harvard professor and an expert in biomedical ethics, says he is expressing the opinion of 'most of those in responsible roles—embryologists, placentologists, foetologists' when he declares, 'We realize that the womb is a dark and dangerous place, a hazardous environment. We should want our potential children to be where they can be watched and protected as much as possible.'[13] With *in vitro* fertilization, transparent artificial wombs and the medical surveillance of gestation, reproduction must become a matter for men, for specialists; it must be rationalized, normalized, denaturalized and, above all, women—whom society has always regarded as irrational beings, ruled by feelings and passions—must be dispossessed once and for all of the powers maternity confers on the mother over her children and the powers it may possibly give her in society. This dispossession, the abolition pure and simple of pregnancy and motherhood, will be achieved, adds Fletcher, with cloning: 'When cloning becomes fully operational for humans, ectogenesis would in some situations eliminate the reimplantation stage to advantage.'[14]

The concern displayed by Fletcher, among others, to eliminate chance (and, more fundamentally, contingency) by eliminating nature, shows up the affinity that exists from the outset between the spirit of science and the spirit of capitalism.[15] For both, nature is first a source of randomness, risk and disorder. It has to be tamed, dominated and, if possible, abolished by a rational *ordering* of the world that eradicates its uncertainties and unpredictabilities. Hostility to chance, hostility to life, hostility to nature—'Order and Progress', as Auguste Comte had it. 'Inner nature' has to be eliminated, as has external nature; both have to be replaced by machinic human beings and human machines within a preprogrammed, self-regulated world-machine. This was the nineteenth-century ideal of the alliance between science and capital in a civilization of engineers. That ideal has been radicalized. The aim now is to (re)create the world—not to order it, but the foundations of that alliance, the affinity between the spirit of capital and the spirit of science, still remain and they allow science to go on towards its goal of achieving autonomy.

In this regard, the plan to achieve ectogenesis—and subsequently, as we shall see, artificial intelligence and artificial life—is paradigmatic. The aim is no less than to *industrialize* the (re)production of humans in the same way as biotechnology is industralizing the (re)production of animal and plant species with the ultimate aim of substituting artificial species created by genetic engineering for the natural ones. The abolition of nature is driven not by the demiurgic project of science but by capital's project for supplanting primal forms of wealth, which nature offers at no cost and which are accessible to all, by artificial, commodity forms—the project of transforming the world into commodities, whose production will be monopolized by capital, which will thus set itself up as ruler of humanity.

We already have a market in sperm, a market in human eggs, a maternity market (the renting of the womb of surrogate mothers), a market in genes, in stem cells, in embryos and a (clandestine) market in bodily organs. The continuation of this trend will lead to the marketing of (allegedly) genetically 'improved' children of all ages, then of cloned or entirely artificial humans or 'post-humans' and of artificial ecological niches on this planet or some other.

Capital and science are using each other in pursuit of their respective goals which, though different, have much in common. Both are pursuing pure 'power' in the sense of Aristotle's *dunamis*, without any other goal but itself. Both are entirely indifferent to any determinate end or need, since nothing equates with the indeterminate power of money on the one hand, and of theoretical knowledge on the other—these being capable of any determination because they reject them all. Both lock themselves off, by the de-subjectivizing techniques of calculation, against the possibility of reflexive contemplation. But some cracks have recently appeared in the alliance between capital and science. For though there is no question for capital of freeing itself from its dependence on science, the prospect is emerging of science being able to free itself from capitalism.

This is the issue emerging on the horizon of the research into artificial intelligence and life, which could potentially usher in a post-natural, post-biological, post-human civilization. This new era first announced itself—though this initially passed without notice—in the mid-twentieth century with the invention by Claude Shannon and Alan Turing of the first 'machines capable of imitating the brain' and, as it was thought, capable of surpassing it. It announced itself further with the virtually simultaneous discovery of the structure of DNA, which would lead Robert Sinsheimer to say, 'We might say that we have discovered the language in which God created life.'[16] Natural history seemed to be approaching its end: 'Man' was to become the 'co-creator, alongside God, of the universe', including life and himself. Science, says V. Elving Anderson, is 'carrying out the divine mandate'.[17]

From that point, science was to become aware of the original sense of its project and dare plainly to express its contempt, if not indeed disgust, for biological life and nature. One of the most significant books in this connection is *The World, the Flesh and the Devil* (1969) by J. D. Bernal, the biologist and British pioneer of X-ray crystallography, who made a decisive contribution to understanding the molecular structure of DNA. In that work, Bernal explains that nature, the body, desires and emotions are the enemies of 'the rational soul':

> The cardinal tendency of progress is the replacement of an indifferent chance environment by a deliberately created one. As time goes on, the acceptance, the appreciation, even the understanding of nature, will be less and less needed. In its place will come the need to determine the desirable form of the humanly-controlled universe.[18]

Though not, apparently, controlled by all those who make up current humanity—Bernal envisages the formation of a scientific elite of men transformed 'in a way quite transcending the capacities of untransformed humanity'. Leaving their bodies far behind, these would be disembodied, virtually immortal minds, equipped with 'mechanized bodies'. 'Normal man is an evolutionary dead end; mechanical man, apparently a break in organic evolution, is actually more in the true tradition of a further evolution.' But the 'new life which conserves none of the substance and all of the spirit of the old' will itself be merely an intermediate phase. 'Finally, consciousness itself may end or vanish in a humanity that has become completely etherealized, losing the close-knit organism, becoming masses of atoms in space communicating by radiation, and ultimately perhaps resolving itself entirely into light.'[19]

FROM ARTIFICAL INTELLIGENCE TO ARTIFICIAL LIFE

We shall come upon this phantasm of an ethereal, immortal spirit 30 years later among the pioneers of artificial intelligence (AI), particularly in the work of Hans Moravec. The first research into the development of machines capable of imitating and surpassing human thought had been carried out at MIT and the RAND Corporation and financed by the Pentagon's Defense Advanced Research Projects Agency (DARPA). The official launch of the AI programme took place at a conference at Dartmouth College in 1956. The conference proposed to take as the basis of its research 'the hypothesis that every aspect of learning or any other feature of intelligence can be so precisely described that a machine can be made to simulate it'.

The conference and the later work were dominated by the personality of Marvin Minsky, who displayed his contempt and disgust for that 'meat machine' the brain and for the 'bloody mess' that is the human body. The mind, in his view, could be separated from the body and the self: 'The important thing in refining your thought is to try to depersonalize your interior.' Like Newell and Simon, he could see no difference between the computers 'that manufacture thoughts' and the human mind; both belong to 'the same species'—stored-programme machines. 'Our brains themselves are machines [. . .] Our mind-engineering skills could grow to the point of enabling us to construct accomplished artificial scientists, artists, composers and personal companions.'[20]

The idea that the immortal 'soul' or 'spirit' can be uploaded to live forever in cyberspace, that the fleshly body is on the point of becoming obsolete and that 'we are like gods' appeared in California in the late 1970s. In 1984, Sherry Turkle published a landmark volume of interviews with researchers.[21] Most of those interviewed were convinced that the intelligence of machines would surpass that of human beings, that machines would free themselves from their dependency on humans and that humans would only be able to preserve their supremacy by living in symbiosis with them. One of the DARPA researchers declared: 'I have a dream to create my own robot. To give it my intelligence. To make it my mind [. . .] to see myself in it [. . .] It is, as a fellow researcher concurred, "the most important thing anyone could do".'[22] Another, an eminent pioneer of AI and the CEO of Thinking Machines Inc., said of his potential double: 'I want to make a machine that will be proud of me.'[23]

The belief in the possibility of transferring the human mind on to an inorganic medium of microcircuitry actually developed as a by-product of military research. In the beginning, the aim was to create a centre that would decode information from the radar surveillance system called SAGE, based in the American Far North, which is intended to indicate the approach of enemy aeroplanes. The F14 jet fighter was subsequently fitted with such an advanced weapons system and such a rapid flow of information on the location of targets, that the use of this information exceeded human capacities. The pilots were to 'improve' their abilities thanks to their symbiosis with computers.

The idea not just of a computer-assisted intellect but of transferring the intellect to computers reaches imaginative maturity in the work of Moravec, who developed advanced robots for NASA. First in *Mind Children* and, subsequently, in *Robot*, Moravec envisages the possibility of 'transplanting' the mind by wiring the neural nets of the brain to a computer, which would make it possible, he writes, for the mind to be 'rescued from the limitations of a mortal body', to be stored in a computer, to have an unlimited number of copies made and to be resuscitated at will.[24]

This naive belief that the brain 'contains' the whole of the mind in the form of a programme that can be transferred and copied like a software package is not unique to Moravec. We have already seen it in Bernal, for whom 'the brain is all that counts' and can operate when detached from the body. We see it in Edward Fredkin (of MIT and Stanford), who believes in the possibility of devising a 'global algorithm' that will lead to 'peace and harmony' on earth and who sees the creation of AI, after that of the universe and life, as the third and last stage of evolution, the stage in which the mind frees itself from the physical universe, and creator and creature will be one.

From the outset, the AI pioneers had defined the human mind as being, like the computer, a 'stored-programme machine'. They had defined thought as a sequence of operations which Bernal foresaw, from the early 1950s, as being susceptible to analysis and transcription by binary arithmetic or, in other words, by the yes/no sequences that make up a computer programme. They went on to demonstrate that practically all problems could be solved if they were transcribed (and transcribable) in this way; that 'thinking machines' could classify, coordinate, memorize and process a greater flow of information more quickly and more reliably than the human intellect; that their capacities of calculation and forecasting were, or could be, far superior, as could even be their capacity for interpretation—on condition, admittedly, that the relations of meaning had been predefined unambiguously.

But they had never asked themselves the central question about the ability to define the problems that were to be solved; to distinguish what is important from what is not, what has meaning from what does not; to choose, define and pursue a goal, to modify it in the light of unforeseen events; and, more fundamentally, the question of the reasons and criteria on the basis of which the goals, problems and solutions are chosen. On what are these choices and these criteria dependent? If intelligence operates like a stored-programme machine, who defined the programme? The AI pioneers had quite simply left aside these questions, which relate to the existence of a living, *con-*

scious subject that thinks, calculates, chooses, acts and pursues goals because she *feels* needs, desires, fears, hopes, pains and pleasures—in short, because she is a *being of needs* and desires who always lacks something that she does not have or does not yet have and who, by dint of her sense of lack, of her sense of *incompleteness*, always feels herself as something yet to come, incapable of coinciding with herself in the still plenitude of a being that simply is what it is.[25]

The pioneers of AI are quite clearly filled with this sense of incompleteness. It is an ontological structure of consciousness. But we must add—of consciousness insofar as it is indissociable from the factuality of one's body; of that consciousness which, from birth, has felt hunger, thirst, cold, and the need for affection and protection. The sense of lacking something, the need to go beyond oneself and satisfy that lack are part of what makes up consciousness. It is on this base that the intelligence develops and from it that it draws its initial drive to live. The machinic conception of intelligence assumes it is something always already there, programmed into the brain, ready to be mobilized. But the intelligence is precisely not a programme that has already been written: it exists as living intelligence only as the capacity to *produce itself* in accordance with its own *intentions*; and this capacity to make oneself into a lack, which underlies the capacity to create, imagine, doubt and change—in a word, to determine oneself—cannot be written into a software programme. It is not programmable because the brain is not a set of written transcribable programmes—it is the living organ of a living body, an organ *that is constantly programming and reprogramming itself.*

Moravec has discovered all this in his own way. Like the other AI pioneers, his initial hypothesis was that intelligence transcribed into digital language would be freed from its body, its factuality, its finitude. But his effort to conceive such an intelligence demonstrated, despite his intentions, that *an intelligence 'liberated' from the life of the body is an intelligence without desire, intentionality, emotions or temporality*; it is pure power without object, differing from nothingness as little as can be, as Valéry puts it. That intelligence does not *live*, does not *exist*.

In *Mind Children*, therefore, Moravec imagined it as a kind of cosmic radiation, outside of time, spreading throughout the universe, 'converting nonlife into mind', and potentially 'convert[ing] the entire universe into an extended thinking entity, a prelude to even greater things'.[26]

However, if intelligence is to exist, to operate in space and time and be capable of learning and acquiring experience, it needs a living body. More exactly, it needs to equip itself with or create its body, to create its life, in a manner appropriate to it. In order to create Artificial Intelligence, one has, then, to create Artificial Life (AL). The research of the AI pioneers, Moravec in particular,[27] but also Raymond Kurzweil, will increasingly turn to robotics and to the design of machines presenting all the characteristics of living intelligence and life: the capacity to sustain and repair themselves, to grow and evolve, to beget, reproduce or create themselves. These are all things which mean that, as Edgar Morin pointed out, life is, first and foremost, *autopoiesis*; it is reducible to nothing else and explicable in no other terms: it is self-explanatory.[28]

The origins of the AL programme lay in John von Neumann's theory of self-reproducing cellular automata. NASA became interested in this after 1980. Its aim was to design factories capable of reproducing themselves, growing, repairing themselves and evolving. The plan was for these entirely autonomous, multi-purpose factories to be installed on other planets, whence they would make it possible to 'take over the entire universe'. In 1985, the US Air Force decided to create its own research centre on AL at Los Alamos, where von Neumann had spent the latter part of his life designing nuclear weapons. The first Los Alamos conference on AL in 1987 defined its mission in the following terms:

> Artificial life is the study of artificial systems
> that exhibit behaviour characteristic of nat-

ural living systems [. . .] Microelectronic technology and genetic engineering will soon
give us the capability to create new life *in
silico* as well as *in vitro*.

The ambitions of the AL pioneers will turn out
to be much grander than this: their aim is to abolish
human nature and the human species in order to create a robotic 'supercivilization', a species 'beyond humanity' that will shape the universe in its image, and
'will [. . .] enable human beings to change into something else altogether'.[29]

FROM THE OBSOLESCENCE OF THE BODY
TO THE END OF THE HUMAN SPECIES

From the Man-Machine to Human Machines

The feasibility and seriousness of the futuristic visions
outlined by the pioneers of AL are of little consequence. All that matters is the sense of their project,
the scientific spirit it reflects. It apparently reflected
that spirit so convincingly that some illustrious representatives of the American intellectual elite have

debated in all seriousness the philosophical questions and ethical problems posed by the vision of a post-biological and post-human civilization (if one dares call it such), dominated by robots superior in every way to human beings.

Put forward by members of elite universities who are uncontested leaders in their disciplines, the projects linking AI and AL, genetic engineering and the nanotechnologies, are presented as the ultimate stage in the fundamental scientific project—to emancipate mind from nature and from the human condition. The proponents of this project lend a neo-Hegelian, Nietzschean or spiritualist cast to its formulation. We must relocate their formulations in the present age to understand that the fundamental project (or 'spirit') of science has successfully (*dared to*) become self-aware. In all its formulations and implications, this project is, in fact, inseparable from the hyper- and postmodern spirit, which sees self-determination, equality, freedom, rights and the dignity of the human person as contemptible Judaeo-Christiano-Kantian relics. The

enterprise that seeks to free intelligence from its biological limitations and the contingency of its genetic
inheritance is not a violation of the laws of nature but,
according to those pioneering it, the exact opposite—
in man, nature has given itself the being through
whom it attains consciousness of itself and makes itself capable of (re-)creating itself and becoming self-
founding. The creation of artificial life and artificial
intelligence is simply, they tell us, the *final act* of evolution through which nature comes into possession of
itself by way of man, to whom nature lent the power
for such a feat. Technology must be understood as nature creating itself through human mediation. Nature
is becoming knowledge and knowledge is becoming
nature. The difference between Being and Thought
(between being and thinking) is disappearing.

These theorizations aren't the mere ideological
trappings of a scientific enterprise pursuing earthly
goals—they regard themselves as the meaning and
primary wellspring of that enterprise. Questions such
as, 'What is the point of all this?', 'What benefits can

humanity derive from it?', 'What civilization and society does science have in store for us?' and 'According to what criteria does it want to recreate human
beings, life and nature?' are seen as trifling concerns
that invalidate the questioners' positions. The pioneers
of AI and AL locate themselves from the outset
above that humanity that crawls along the ground.
They take the view that the biological evolution of
mankind is a dead end (Kurzweil) and that the development of intelligence on a technological basis is dictated by the laws of evolution. In a sense, for them
evolution uses humanity to transcend human intelligence. 'The path is marked out,' says Kurzweil. 'We
have no choice.' And Moravec sees the robots of the
future explicitly as the bearers of a mind that transcends that of man. Hugo de Garis sees himself as
the 'fourth and darkest horseman of the Apocalypse,
the one of the war' which the robots who emancipate
themselves from it will wage against the human race.[30]

All declare themselves convinced that, in the
course of the twenty-first century, the world will be

dominated by intelligent machines and that 'humans, if they still exist, will be subservient.'[31] They are all convinced that, as a result of Moore's Law, the processing power of computers will have increased by a factor of 10^6 by around 2020 or 2030 and that 'the robots coming out of the laboratories will dominate the ones that designed them.'[32] By around the same date, nanotechnologies will enable us, asserts Kurzweil, to create 'nanobots' on the scale of a molecule which, 'when sent into the brain by the blood flow, will copy it synapse by synapse and neurotransmitter by neurotransmitter.' It will then be possible, says Kurzweil, to create exact copies of the human brain and to augment its intelligence by adding 'billions of artificial neurons'. And since the intelligence of biological humanity evolves only slowly, whereas 'machine intelligence grows exponentially', machines 'will soon be much more intelligent than human beings', and human beings, so as not to be dominated by them, will be forced to incorporate increasing quantities of artificial neurons into their nervous systems. 'In the long run, the non-biological component of our intelligence will become dominant. We shall have machine creatures that are entirely non-biological but [. . .] will give the impression of being absolutely human.'[33]

All in all, then, to be able to control their robots, endowed with greatly superior intelligence, human beings will be forced to transform themselves into robots. The difference between human robots and robotic humans will tend to disappear.

All this 'evolution' is presented by Kurzweil and his colleagues as inevitable and natural. It will bring about the end of currently existing human societies. In his book, Kurzweil quotes at length from the *Manifesto* of Theodore Kaczynski (alias 'The Unabomber'). In a tightly argued passage, Kaczysnki demonstrates that humans will be led, willy-nilly, to abandon their decision-making power entirely to machines gradually and without realizing it, since a world in which large-scale systems of intelligent machines assume wider and wider functions will become so complex that only machines will be able to manage it. In these conditions, will the control of intelligent machines with powers to coordinate, manage and regulate material and immaterial flows still be possible? It is not at all certain that it will. What is sure is that only a 'tiny elite' will perhaps have the necessary skills to control and steer the big machine-intelligence-based systems. The power of that elite over the 'masses' will be total, since human labour will have become superfluous. The 'mass' of human beings will have become a useless burden on the system. The elite will have the choice either to exterminate them or to 'reduce them to the status of domestic animals' by occupying them in an-odine entertainments, writes Kaczynski. Or alternatively, through mind-control by sending 'nanobots' into the brains of a useless humanity.[34]

Kurzweil himself sees the technological elite as a 'praetorian guard', a caste of 'high-tech high priests' guiding the rest of humanity. The development of society and civilization is thus entirely subordinated to the development of thinking machines. De Garis is certain that these machines will push out humans after winning the war with them. He opts for their side in that war. Moravec predicts that, in the competition for the control of natural resources, 'biological humans' will in the end be defeated. 'Biological species rarely survive encounters with superior competitors.'[35] The only ones with a chance of surviving are the post-human cyborgs whose non-biological prostheses will enable them to match up to machines.

One way or another, the end of the human race is on the cards. 'Evolution' means mankind must inevitably produce a 'counter-man' that will spell its doom. Science is enacting its original plan—it is freeing itself from the human species.

The sadistic pleasure with which the members of the techno-elite foretell the Apocalypse is most significant. I would not have dared invent this to illustrate the spirit of science—I would have felt I was crudely exaggerating its hatred of nature and life. It seems likely that very many of the post-biological and post-human prophecies will turn out to be infantile fantasies and that AI and AL will not fulfil the dystopian 'promise' their pioneers see in them. But, for all that, we should not be so reassured. 'The path is marked out,' said Kurzweil. Others will follow it by other means.

Genetic Reprogramming: Of Whom By Whom?

The project of improving the human species goes back a long way. All that has changed is the set of reasons invoked for advocating eugenics. In this connection, Vance Packard quotes a work by Sir Francis Galton, one of the first, nineteenth-century proponents of eugenics: 'It has now become a serious necessity to better the breed of the human race. The average citizen is too base for the everyday work of modern civilization.'[36] The amelioration of the species is a response not to a human need, then, but to the needs of machines. As Bowring notes, the biological constitution of human beings has become 'a hindrance' . . . '*from the point of view of machines*'.[37] Kurzweil says the same thing in a different way: 'In the next [i.e. twenty-first] century, a point will be reached where the knowledge and capacities of an average individual no longer suffice. Whoever wishes to participate in economic life will have to equip his brain with artificial intelligence.'[38] Technoscience, combined with capital, has produced a world that is unliveable for human beings. So human beings have to be changed. This amounts to saying that the machine is king and human beings are merely its subjects.

In *On Behalf of God*, V. Elving Anderson and Bruce Reichenbach declare: '*we* have enormous powers to begin to redesign the kinds of human beings we want on earth [. . .] *we* might be able genetically to tailor future generations to certain broad specifications.'[39] But *who is 'we'*? *Who is redesigning whom* and by what criteria?

For the moment, genetic re-engineering meets the demands of a 'grey market', fuelled by the illusions maintained by 'science' about the determining power of genes.[40] These demands seem normal and plausible because society tacitly accepts or tolerates them. There is a creeping occupation of this terrain by genetic engineering and even the cloning of human beings is presented in a harmless light—why deny biological offspring to people who would not otherwise have them? Why should men or women not be entitled to create their doubles if they so wish?[41] Isn't it normal for parents to want to endow their children with the best possible 'genetic capital'? It is not difficult to guess that 'performance' will come out ahead of all the other hereditary (?) characteristics that genetic engineering will be tasked with boosting, and that this will give powerful leverage to Social Darwinism.

But let us come back to the question of the 'we'. Genetic engineering, like AI and AL, presents itself as a project that will enable 'us' to free 'ourselves' from the contingency of our factuality—'we' are going to recreate and transcend 'ourselves' or even abolish the human condition. This re-creation might be said to be the supreme stage of self-production. But it is a grammatical mirage, for, unlike the self-production in which I 'transform myself by techniques of the self' or 'self-manipulation', as Peter Sloterdijk has it[42] (in such a way that capacities I didn't previously possess may blossom within me as my own, with only the trial-and-error of self-directed learning making it possible for them to develop within me), genetic engineering and AI are not techniques of the self or auto-techniques, but hetero-technologies.[43]

When Morin predicts that 'the power of the mind over genes will soon exceed the power of genes over the mind and the power of the mind over the brain that of the brain over the mind', is he in fact speaking of *my* mind and *my* brain?[44] If he is, there would be nothing very new in this: 'Among the yogis, purely spiritual exercises are successful in deeply controlling the activities of the heart by use of the brain.'[45] To put it more prosaically, I modify and increase the capacities of my brain through all the learning techniques and memory exercises I employ, and by pursuing virtuosity in the mastery of an art or a sport. This is all work by oneself on oneself, work of self-production by 'techniques of the self'. Yet, it is precisely this work of self-production we are going to be spared by replacing it with hetero-techniques of external intervention on the brain and (allegedly) on the genome. 'Science' is proposing that we *have ourselves produced by* licensed specialists, that we become consumers and purchasers of the 'improvement' of our faculties.

Similarly, when Kurzweil predicts that the implantation of billions of artificial neurons will enable 'us' to enhance 'our' intelligence and sensibility, the design and implantation of these neurons will have nothing of a work of self-production about them. If it takes place, the enhancement of these faculties will be the product of a hetero-technical act, with the beneficiary having no work of experimentation and learning to perform. Moreover, when Kurzweil promises that the transfer of information from a software package to a brain will enable someone to read a book in a few seconds and quasi-instantaneously possess a foreign language, he is in fact promising that learning, experience and work on oneself will become superfluous, without asking himself how new *formal knowl-*

edge can be *incorporated* by the person, how it can become experiential knowledge and be converted into practical, active skills; how, for example, the brain can speak Chinese with the mouth of a Swede or play the piano with a boxer's hands. The implicit assumption is that the brain, with its quasi-instantaneously enhanced capacities, will actualize these capacities thanks to prostheses that stand in for bodily knowledge—that it will speak Chinese using a vocal robotic device, play the piano with artificial hands, etc. 'We' shall be cyborgs. The work of self-production will give way to the purchase of prostheses by means of which everyone will be able to transform themselves and enhance themselves indefinitely, to reinvent themselves by merging with machinic extensions of themselves.

And, in fact, the pioneers of AI and the cyborg ideologues warned us—there is, they say, no difference between human subjectivity and that of machines. Software is a subjectivity like any other. 'The machine is not an *it* to be animated, worshipped and dominated. The machine is us, our processes, an aspect of our embodiment,' wrote Donna Haraway in a famous text in 1991.[46] This is to deny the essential difference between biological embodiment and machinic embodiment—through the first native form, we are given to ourselves; it is the natural contingency of the chance occurrence of our birth. The second is manufactured by others for a determinate goal—for example, to procure for us the thrilling experience of great acceleration, high speeds, the contraction of time, or superhuman strength and skill. And it is true that fast cars and intelligent machine-tools are like extensions of our bodies, that we fuse with them when we handle them with virtuosity. But the difference from our biological bodies is that they were designed by others and the enhanced possibilities they afford us *were determined by those others*. They gave us the means to do or be what they imagined we would or should wish to be or do—*we are programmed by them*, or at least predicted by them.[47] As cyborgs, we handle machines forming extensions of our bodies without understanding either their operation or their design. These machines differ from the techniques by which humans have, in the case of every human being, produced themselves as human. We do not produce ourselves by using them—*we have ourselves produced by them*.

The difference between the natural body and the body reprogrammed by science comes into stark relief in the case of genetic engineering. From the standpoint of science, decoding the human genome and the possibility of modifying it should enable us to free humanity from the random effects of the natural lottery that is sexual reproduction. Humanity should be able to choose its future characteristics and programme them. Instead of being the product of chance, the genetic inheritance could be defined, improved and even differentiated at will on the basis of the conscious decisions of 'human beings themselves'. It would be entirely as though nature were becoming self-aware through them and were equipping itself with the means to emancipate its evolution from the effects of chance. The difference between the artificial and the natural, between culture and nature, would be set to disappear.

It matters little here that 'scientific' ideology attributes a power to genes that is at variance with reality. The redefinition of the genetic heritage raises ethical, social and anthropological problems, whether or not it actually has the capacity to fulfil its declared aims. First, though the modification of the genome is indeed the effect of a choice on the part of 'human beings themselves', that choice is not and never will be a choice that humanity can make within every human being. *Those who will choose to reshape human beings—or some human beings—will not be the reshaped human beings themselves.* These latter will not have chosen to be so— they will have been reshaped by virtue of a choice made by others, on the basis of criteria not established by their own judgement. Whatever its intrinsic degree of effectiveness, genetic engineering is, in its essence, a resolve on the part of third parties to predetermine what an as-yet-unborn individual is to become. It will have effects, even if its causal effectiveness is non-existent. Hans Jonas has pointed out this aspect in an article on cloning:

Note that it does not matter one jot whether the genotype is really, by its own force, a person's fate: it is *made* his fate by the very assumptions in cloning him, which by their imposition on all concerned become a force themselves [. . .] Existentially significant is what the cloned individual *thinks*—is compelled to think—of himself, not what he is in the substance-sense of being. In brief, he is antecedently robbed of the *freedom* which only under the protection of ignorance can thrive.[48]

In concrete terms, the parents expect genetic engineering to have a determinate effect on the personality of the child and treat that child in terms of the predispositions the engineering is supposed to produce, in terms of the 'vocation' that is supposed to be hers. What Kant called the 'dictate of birth' will find itself radicalized by this. It will be difficult for the adolescent to understand herself as the author of her own life. She will examine all events and all decisions in the light of her supposed genetic destiny. She will be constantly wondering: was I programmed to take that decision or did I take it freely? Am I possessed by an alien will or am I master of my choices? Jürgen Habermas writes as follows:

> When the adolescent learns about the design drawn up by another person for intervening in her genetic features [. . .] it might usher in the vertiginous awareness that, as a consequence of a genetic intervention carried out before we were born, the subjective nature we experience as being something we cannot dispose over is actually the result of an instrumentalization of a part of our nature [. . .][49]

> The couple that plan the nature of their offspring play a role in their life that the offspring can never play in their own. For the children, when they become adults, 'a form of reciprocal recognition based on strict equality is no longer possible.'[50]

They experience lifelong domination by their parents, a domination inscribed in their genome.

If genetic engineering is left to the parents' initiative, we shall moreover see the development of a market in (supposed) genetic profiles. The outcome will be two human species: the one predestined and 'genetically enhanced'; the other a 'wild' type. Genetic engineering will function as a mechanism of social selection and hierarchization. If, on the other hand, genetic engineering is socialized, it will be a mechanism for normalization and standardization. Whatever the intention with which it is carried out, all citizens will have science and the state as their begetters and co-begetters.

There is no way out of the trap. The uncontrollable chance effects of biology protected us from arbitrary action on the part of human beings. We are the children of chance—not of an alien will. If the lottery of heredity were eliminated, we would be biologically determined by third parties. Whether that predetermination is benevolent or tyrannical, the outcome is the same—the reshapers of the genome insinuate themselves into the deepest level of one's self-understanding. No one will be able to claim he belongs to himself, that he is the product of his work of self-production. The sense each person had of his uniqueness, autonomy and responsibility will be undermined. The main obstacle to the programming and differentiation of individuals to meet the interests of the social order or the dominant class or caste would be abolished. New forms of slavery and new caste systems could be instituted, founded and legitimated by the *belief* in the effectiveness of genetic remodelling, even if that effectiveness did not exist.

Whether social or parental, genetic engineering marks the final abandonment of the principle that 'all men are born equal and free.' It puts an end to the mythic grand narratives that establish the unity of a people and a culture on the founding event that engendered humanity in each of its members. Without a common origin, without the shared understanding of all in each, there are neither society, civilization, founding fathers nor a tradition to pass on. Without

links of kinship or descendence and with no identifi-
able begetters, children will never be certain of having
been brought into the world *because they were desired*;
their existences will always be beset with doubt about
their legitimacy, their right to life and their member-
ship of humanity. Without relations of descendence,
without reference to ancestors, past generations and
legendary founders, there can be no society. Human-
ization is not something assured at birth. It has to be
achieved for and by each individual.[51]

ALLOTECHNOLOGY AND HOMEOTECHNOLOGY: A 'REFORM OF THE MIND'

Only in societies where the potentially hegemonic
sectors no longer see themselves as belonging to any
kind of society have the idea and the project of the
self-begetting of a post-human species been able to
emerge. Reich has spoken of this form of dissidence
among the techno-elite of the 'symbolic analysts'. Sloterdijk offers the same analysis from an anthropological standpoint:

Part of the present human species, under the leadership of the Euro-American factions, has, with its entry into the high-tech era, begun a procedure on itself and against itself, in which a new definition of the human species is at stake.[52]

Further on, he offers this note on how this new definition should not be understood:

The compositions [*Schriftsätze*] of technology [. . .] give rise neither to acclimatization nor to effects of the taming of exteriority. On the contrary, they increase the volume of the exterior and of the forever inassimilable. The province of language shrinks and the sector of machine-readable text expands.[53]

In other words, by dint of treating the world as an external material that is to be subordinated to 'ends that are fundamentally indifferent and alien to it', technoscience, by its 'allotechnologies', has produced a machinized, reified, violated universe that can no longer be lived and experienced as a 'habitat' or 'homeland' for human beings: 'The lack of a home-land [*Heimatlosigkeit*] is the dominant fact of the contemporary *modus essendi*.'[54]

We find a very similar diagnosis, despite the difference in underlying philosophies, in the writings of Morin:

> The human mind has lost control of its creations, science and technology, and has not gained control of its social and historical organizations. The mind controls the increasingly efficient machines it has created, but the logic of these artificial machines is increasingly controlling the minds of the technicians, scientists, sociologists, politicians and, more broadly, all those who, respecting the sovereignty of calculation, take no account of what is not quantifiable—namely, the feelings, sufferings and joys of human beings. This logic is applied to the knowledge and conduct of societies and is spreading

into all areas of life. Artificial intelligence is already in the minds of our leaders and our education system encourages this logic to take a hold on our own minds.

The mind has the greatest power available to it, yet suffers from the greatest infirmity in conditions of greatest power [. . .] The battle is being fought out today on the terrain of the mind. The problem of the reform of thinking or, in other words, the reform of the mind, has become vital.[55]

It is on the reform of thought that Sloterdijk's contribution deserves the greatest attention. He tells us that mankind's relation to the world has been dominated since the Neolithic by 'allotechnologies' or, in other words, by the violation of the nature of things—things regarded as materials, as 'raw materials' to be dominated, 'enslaved' and used for ends that are fundamentally alien to them. With the old concept of matter we invariably assume that, 'given its minimal and, ultimately, recalcitrant aptitudes [*Eignungen*]',[56] it

197

has to be subjugated by force. In a word, allotech-nologies belong to what Jacques Robin calls the 'energy era', an era whose end is nigh from the moment that a previously ignored dimension of matter is disclosed to human intelligence: information. Humanity then enters a new era, the 'information era'.

Sloterdijk's analysis is very close to Robin's.[57] Allotechnology is 'outdated technology' as soon as it becomes clear that 'there is information' in nature, that there are 'self-organizing systems'; that 'mind or thought can insinuate themselves into "the state of things" and remain there,' becoming 'objective memories'.[58] 'Informed matter', intelligent machines or machines 'going as far as the appearance of a planning intelligence and capacity for dialogue', genes that represent 'the purest form of informed and informing matter, since genes are simply "orders" ensuring the synthesis of protein molecules'—all these things invalidate the dualism that rigorously separated 'soul from thing, mind from matter'.[59]

[With the statement] 'there is information,' the old image of technology as heteronomy and the enslavement of materials loses its plausibility [. . .] With intelligent technologies, a non-dominant form of operativity is emerging, for which we propose the name homeotechnology. By its very nature, homeotechnology cannot desire anything utterly different from what the 'things themselves' are or can become of their own accord [. . .] Homeotechnology advances only on the path of the non-violation of being [. . .] It has to rely on cooperative, co-intelligent, co-informative strategies. It has a character of cooperation rather than domination.[60]

The coming of a homeotechnological culture is, however, delayed and thwarted by 'the habitus of violation in relations with the essent in general', by what the proponents of Critical Theory called cognitive-instrumental reason, by 'the alliance between very high technologies and low subjectivity'.[61] 'The habits and compulsions acquired over an entire era, which consist in the aggressive [*vergewaltigenden*] splitting-up of complex relations, will not dissolve overnight.'[62] 'The masters and violators' will tend to resort to 'allotechnological habits in the field of homeotechnology' or, in other words, to treating genes as raw material and using 'anthropoplastic' engineering for purposes of domination.[63] We may expect, adds Sloterdijk, 'that habitus to be proved wrong by its own failures'.[64] But 'we may also ask ourselves whether homeotechnological thinking—which has so far been spoken of under such headings as ecology and the science of complexity—has the potential to unleash an ethics based on relationships free of enmity and domination.'[65]

This amounts to admitting that the long-term failure Sloterdijk predicts for the masters and violators will not, of itself, bring about 'the reform of thought that has become vitally essential'. There is a danger that it will first lead to the coming of monsters and the end of the human species. Who, then, will wage the necessary 'battle of minds'?

Notes

1 Edmund Husserl, 'Einleitung in die Logik und Erkenntnistheorie' (Introduction to Logic and Epistemology), lectures from 1906 to 1907, *Gesammelte Werke*, VOL. 24 (Dordrecht: Springer Netherlands, 1985), p. 182. Cited in Rudolf Boehm, *Topik* (Dordrecht: Kluwer Academic Publishers, 2002), p. 66. This work is a continuation of Boehm's *Kritik der Grundlagen des Zeitalters* (Critique of the Foundations of the Age; The Hague: Martinus Nijhoff, 1974).

2 André Gorz, 'Political Ecology between Expertocracy and Self-Limitation', *Ecologica* (London/New York/Calcutta: Seagull Books, 2010), pp. 43–76. First published in *Actuel Marx* 12 (1992).

3 Bensayag and Sztulwark, *Du contre-pouvoir*, pp. 110–11.

4 Ibid., p. 111.

5 Finn Bowring, *Science, Seeds and Cyborgs*: *Biotechnology and the Appropriation of Life* (London: Verso, 2003), p. 274. The quotation from George Dyson is taken from *Darwin Among the Machines* (London: Penguin, 1997), p. 209.

6 This concern to crossfertilize culture with science was the original programme of the journal *Transversales Science Culture*, the founders of which, grouped around

Jacques Robin, had connections with the pioneers of systems theory.

7 Edmund Husserl, *The Crisis of European Sciences and Transcendental Phenomenology* (Evanston: Northwestern University Press, 1970). The first part of this work was published in 1936 in the Belgrade-based journal *Philosophia* 1(1–4).

8 See George Boole, *An Investigation in the Laws of Thought on which are founded the Mathematical Theories of Logic and Probabilities* (Dover: Walton and Maberly, 1854).

9 In David F. Noble, *The Religion of Technology: The Divinity of Man and the Spirit of Invention* (London: Penguin, 1999), p. 152. Noble is glossing Turing's use of the expression 'the transmigration of souls' in his paper 'Computing Machinery and Intelligence', *Mind* 59 (1963).

10 Raymond Kurzweil, *The Age of Spiritual Machines* (London: Phoenix, 1999).

11 *Selected Writings of Paul Valéry* (Anthony Bower and J. Laughlin eds) (New York: New Directions Publishing Corporation, 1950), p. 91. I take this phrase from the 'Note et Digression' in Paul Valéry's *Variété I* (Paris: Gallimard, 1924) that precedes the 'Introduction to the

Method of Leonardo da Vinci'. In this admirable text, written in 1919, Valéry, without realizing it, carries out the first analysis by phenomenological reduction of the being of consciousness. He describes it as non-coincidence with self, whatever one may do; as continuous creation; as acute awareness of the contingency of one's factuality ('It dares to consider its body and its world as almost arbitrary restrictions imposed on the range of its functions.'—*Selected Writings*, p. 90) and of the contingency of the existent ('The wonder is not that things should be; it is that there should be such things and not such other things.'—Ibid.).

12 Coinciding with oneself as total indeterminacy, as 'absence of project', with regard to which any determination is a 'downfall', is the central theme of the spiritual exercises that are Georges Bataille's *Inner Experience* (New York: State University of New York Press, 1988) and *Le Coupable* (Paris: Gallimard, 1944).

13 Joseph Fletcher, *The Ethics of Genetic Control*: *Ending Reproductive Roulette* (Buffalo: Prometheus Books, 1988). Cited in Bowring, *Science, Seeds and Cyborgs*, p. 244. On the overtly anti-feminine character of science, see 'The Masculine Millennium' in Noble, *The Religion of Technology*, pp. 209–28.

14 Fletcher, *The Ethics of Genetic Control.*

15 I use the expression 'spirit of science' in a Weberian sense, not in the sense of the 'scientific mind'.

16 Robert Sinsheimer, *The Strands of Life* (Berkeley: University of California Press, 1943), p. 3.

17 V. Elving Anderson is professor of genetics at the University of Minnesota and is the author, with Bruce Reichenbach, of *On Behalf of God: A Christian Ethic for Biology* (Grand Rapids: William Eerdman, 1995). Cited in Noble, *The Religion of Technology*, p. 196.

18 J. D. Bernal, *The World, the Flesh and the Devil: An Enquiry into the Future of the Three Enemies of the Rational Soul* (Bloomington: Indiana University Press, 1969), p. 42 et seq.

19 Cf. Hans Moravec, *Robot: Mere Machine to Transcendent Mind* (New York: Oxford University Press, 1999).

20 Marvin Minsky, 'Thoughts about Artificial Intelligence' in Raymond Kurzweil (ed.), *The Age of Intelligent Machines* (Cambridge: Massachussets Institute of Technology Press, 1990). Cited in Noble, *The Religion of Technology*, p. 157.

21 Sherry Turkle, *The Second Self* (New York: Simon and Schuster, 1984).

22 Cited in Noble, *The Religion of Technology*, p. 160.

23 Ibid., p. 163.

24 Hans Moravec, *Mind Children: The Future of Robot and Human Intelligence* (Cambridge and London: Harvard University Press), p. 122.

25 See Jean-Paul Sartre, *Being and Nothingness* (London: Methuen, 1972), pp. 73–105.

26 Moravec, *Mind Children*, p. 116.

27 Moravec is the director and co-founder of the Mobile Robot Laboratory at Carnegie-Mellon University, the biggest centre in the world for research into robotics.

28 See Edgar Morin, *La Vie de la vie* (The Life of Life; Paris: Le Seuil, 1980).

29 Earl Cox and Gregory Paul, *Beyond Humanity: Cyber-Revolution and Future Mind* (Cambridge: Charles River Media, 1996), pp. 1–7.

30 Hugo de Garis, Interview in *Le Monde Interactif* (27 September 2000).

31 Kevin Warwick, *In the Mind of the Machine: The Breakthrough in Artificial Intelligence* (London: Arrow, 1998), p. 261.

32 De Garis, Interview in *Le Monde Interactif.*

33 'der nichtbiologische Teil unseres Verstands [wird] auf
   Dauer dominieren. Wir werden Meschenwesen haben,
   die ganz und gar nichtbiologisch sind, aber [. . .] sie werden absolut menschlich wirken.'—Kurzweil, cited in
   Christian Tenbrock, 'Was bleibt vom Menschen?' (What
   Remains of the Human Being?), *Die Zeit* 16 (11 No-
   vember 1999).

34 In Kurzweil, *The Age of Spiritual Machines*, pp. 179–80.

35 Moravec, *Robot*, p. 134.

36 Cited in Vance Packard, *The People Shapers* (London:
   Futura Publications, 1978), p. 255.

37 Bowring, *Science, Seeds and Cyborgs*, p. 274.

38 'Im nächsten Jahrhundert wird ein Punkt erreicht werden, an dem das Wissen und die Fähigkeiten eines
   Durchschnittsmenschen nicht mehr ausreichen. Wer
   dann am Wirtschaftsleben teilnehmen will, wird sein
   Gehirn mit künstlicher Intelligenz aufrüsten müssen.'
   —Kurzweil, cited in Tenbrock, 'Was bleibt vom Menschen?'

39 Anderson and Reichenbach, *On Behalf of God*, cited in
   Noble, *The Religion of Technology*, p. 197. Emphasis mine
   [A.G.].

40 See the magisterial demystification of the role of genes in the transmission of hereditary characteristics by J. J. Kupiec and P. Sonigo, *Ni Dieu ni gène. Pour une autre théorie de l'hérédité* (Neither God nor Gene. Argument for Another Theory of Hereditary; Paris: Le Seuil, 2000). See also Chapter 6 ('Health and Disease: the Limitations of Genetic Determinism') in Bowring, *Science, Seeds and Cyborgs*.

41 In the surveys carried out in the USA, the infantile desire to have a double is frequently invoked by advocates of the legalization of cloning.

42 See Peter Sloterdijk, 'Domestikation des Seins' (Domestication of Being) in *Nicht gerettet. Versuche nach Heidegger* (Frankfurt: Suhrkamp, 2001).

43 Gorz plays here on an opposition between the terms 'autotechnique' and 'hétérotechnique'. The term autotechnique seems, however, to have been created by Olivier Mannoni to translate Sloterdijk's 'Selbsttechnik', which is itself a German translation of Foucault's 'technique de soi'. I have attempted a translation that does not add further to these 'Chinese whispers'. [Trans.]

44 Edgar Morin, *L'Humanité de l'humanité* (The Humanity of Humanity; Paris: Le Seuil, 2002), pp. 242–43.

45 Ibid.

46 Donna Haraway, 'A Cyborg Manifesto: Science, Technology and Socialist-Feminism in the Late Twentieth Century' in *Simians, Cyborgs and Women: The Reinvention of Nature* (London: Free Association Books, 1991), p. 180.

47 This is one of the fertile ideas of Ivan Illich: in *Tools for Conviviality* (New York: Harper & Row, 1973), he dubs those tools convivial that do not programme their use or their users, and heteronomous those which do so.

48 Hans Jonas, 'Biological Engineering—A Preview' in *Philosophical Essays: From Ancient Creed to Technological Man* (Englewood Cliffs, NJ: Prentice Hall, 1974), pp. 161–62. Emphasis in the original [A. G.].

49 Jürgen Habermas, *The Future of Human Nature* (Cambridge: Polity, 2003), pp. 53–4. See also Jacques Robin, *Changer d'ère* (Paris: Le Seuil, 1989), p. 169 et seq.

50 Habermas, *The Future of Human Nature*, p. 82.

51 This theme is developed by Monette Vacquin in *Main basse sur les vivants* (Life-Grab; Paris: Fayard, 1999), Chapter 15 and Conclusion.

52 Sloterdijk, 'Domestikation des Seins', p. 165.

53 Ibid., pp. 212–13.

54 Ibid., p. 213.

55 Morin, *L'Humanité de l'humanité*, pp. 242–3.

56 Sloterdijk, 'Domestikation des Seins', p. 226.

57 See Robin, *Changer d'ère*, pp. 227, 314–20.

58 Sloterdijk, 'Domestikation des Seins', p. 218.

59 Ibid., pp. 220–1.

60 Ibid., pp. 227–8

61 Ibid., pp. 229–30.

62 Ibid., p. 232

63 Ibid., pp. 230–1.

64 Ibid., p. 233.

65 Ibid., p. 231.